Passenger Liners from Germany
1816-1990

Clas Broder Hansen

Passenger Liners from Germany 1816-1990

1469 Morstein Road, West Chester, Pennsylvania 19380

The frontispiece shows the high-speedliner *Bremen* (see pp. 149-153) in the spring of 1939, during a cruise around South America; she is shown before the Gatun Locks of the Panama Canal, which she was the largest ship to pass through to that time.

Photo credits: Berliner Verlag photo archives (pp, 170 below, 171, 174 above), Prussian Kulturbesitz photo archives (pp. 10 below, 14 below, 29), Süddeutsche Verlag photo archives (pp. 2, 58, 59 above, 86 lower left, 116 above, 119, 123, 128 below, 136 below, 146 above, 154 above and below, 156 upper left, right and below, 161 above), Blohm & Voss AG (pp. 45 above, 68 above, upper and lower center, 69 above, 76 above and below, 77 above and below, 82 above, 83, 100-101, 112-113, 114, 115 above, center and below, 156 upper left, 162 above and center, 163 above), Bremen State Museum of Art and Cultural History/Focke Museum (pp. 16, 23 above and below), Hans Breuer/State Photo Department, Hamburg (pp. 111, 114 above and below), Harro Christiansen (pp. 57 above, 71 above, 122)Color-Dia-Verlag Hans Hartz (pp. 135 above, 168 below, 178 above, 179 below, 182 above), German Museum (pp. 12, 14 above, 42 below, 43 below, 146 below), German Maritime Museum (pp. 34 below, 35 above, 42 above, 51 below, 72 above, 134 center and below, 136 above, 150-151, 155, 156 upper right, 159 above, 163 below, 175, 179 center, 186 above and center, 188 above and below), Cassen Eils (p. 179 above), Jürgen Fensch (p. 170 above), Wolfgang Fuchs (pp. 145, 148, 166 below, 173, 185 below, 187 above), Johanna & Heinrich Hamann/State Photo Department, Hamburg (pp. 38, 39, 62 below, 73 below, 74, 75, 80 above and below, 88 below, 97, 98, 104 above and below, 105, 165), Hamburg-South American Steamship Co. Eggert & Amsinck (pp. 49 above and below, 50 below, 51 above, 68 below, 110 below, 124 above and below, 126, 129, 142, 143), Clas Broder Hansen (pp. 185 center, 187 below), Hapag-Lloyd AG (pp. 22 below, 31, 32 above and below, 33 above and below, 34 above and below, 35 below, 40, 41, 42 center, 44 above and below, 45 above and below, 46 above and below, 47 above and below, 48, 50 above, 52, 53, 54 below, 55, 57 above, 62 above, 63, 67 above, 69 below, 70 above, 71 center and below, 73 above and center, 78 above and below, 79, 84 above, 85 above and below, 86 upper left and right, 87, 88 above, 90, 91, 95 above, center and below, 102, 103 above and below, 106, 107, 108, 109, 110 above, 116 below, 117 above and below, 118 above and below, 120 above and below, 121, 128 below, 132, 133, 138, 139, 141, 159 below, 164, 167, 168 above and center, 175 below), Husum Ship-yards (p. 178 below), P. A. Krochnert (pp. 181, 189), Herbert Kuke (pp. 13, 147 below, 185 above), Hero Lang (pp. 64 above, 153, 158 above, 160, 166 above, 177, 180, 184, 187 center), Museum of Hamburg History (pp. 11, 17, 24), private parties (pp. 54 above, 61, 64 below, 65, 66, 81, 84 below, 94, 156 lower left and right), Dr. K. Rolle, p. 172 above), F. J. H. Schepers (p. 173 below), Rostock Maritime Museum (pp. 18 below, 70 below), Rob. M. Sloman, Jr. (p. 20), State Photo Department, Hamburg (pp. 30, 37, 162 below, 179 below, 182 below), City Photo Archives, Cuxhaven (pp. 36, 43 above, 60, 67 below, 112 above, 129, 134 above, 158 below, 178 center), Dieter Steffen (p. 176), TT Line (pp. 174 below, 186 below), Ullstein Picture Service (pp. 82 below, 99, 149), Verkehrsmuseum Nürnberg archives (pp. 15, 18 above, 59 below, 72 below, 183), Jutta Vialon (p. 169).

All other illustrations came from the archives of Urbes Verlag.

Translated from the German by Dr. Edward Force,
Central Connecticut State University.

Copyright © 1991 by Schiffer Publishing Ltd.
Library of Congress Catalog Number: 91-65662

Printed in the United States of America.
ISBN: 0-88740-325-5

This title was originally published under the title, *Die Deutschen Passagierschiffe 1816-1990*, by Urbes Verlag, Munich. 1990.
ISBN: 3-924896-19-4.

We are interested in hearing from authors with book ideas on related topics.

Published by Schiffer Publishing, Ltd.
1469 Morstein Road
West Chester, Pennsylvania 19380
Please write for a free catalog.
This book may be purchased from the publisher.
Please include $2.00 postage.
Try your bookstore first.

Foreword

This book is intended to present an overview showing the development of the German passenger ship from its origin to the present. Thus it fills a gap, for such a complete portrayal in one volume has not existed to date. The main subjects are the great oversea steamships, particularly the famous transatlantic liners, as well as every important German passenger ship; a thorough treatment of German passenger shipping also includes, on the one hand, those early steamers that formed the fastest and most important means of passenger transport within Germany for some three decades, before the building of the railroad lines, and on the other, the sea resort ships running in coastal waters, the Baltic and North Sea ferries and the railroad ships, as long as they were not purely freight carriers, and thus their history is also considered in this volume.

The compiling of this book with its numerous historical illustrations, most of them never before published, would not have been possible without the encouragement and advice, the shared information and energetic support to those for which thanks are due: Elke Barg of the Focke Museum in Bremen, A.K. Beken in Cowes, Professor Högele of the Bodensee District of the German Federal Railways Shipping Department in Konstanz, Dr. Dirk Böndel of the Museum of Transit and Technology in Berlin, Hermann Borrmann of the Cuxhaven City Archives, Reinhold Breden in Bremerhaven, Dipl.Ing. Jobst Broelmann of the German Museum in Munich, Eduard Bündgen in Köln, M. Burmeister of the Ostsee-Zeitung in Rostock, Beate Christians of the State Photo Department in Hamburg, Harro Christiansen of Blohm & Voss AG in Hamburg, Ursula Cosmann of the Markish Museum in Berlin, Uwe Diers of the German African Line in Hamburg, Werner Dobras of the City Archives in Lindau, John Gerrit Edye of the Rob. M. Sloman Jr. firm in Hamburg, Mr. Ehmann of the Middle Rhenish Museum in Koblenz, Rolf Finck of Hapag-Lloyd AG in Hamburg, Bernd Franke of the Reederei Cassen Eils in Cuxhaven, Wolfgang Fuchs in Hamburg, Mr. Groebler of the AG Reederei Norden-Frisia in Norden, Kurt Groggert in Berlin, Mrs. Hartz in Hamburg, Mrs. Heidt of the Süddeutsche Verleg in Munich, Mr. Hilmer in Munich, Werner Hinsch of the Elbe Maritime Museum in Lauenburg, Dr. Norbert Humburg of the Hameln Museum, Mr. Illenseer of the Transport Museum archives in Nürnberg, Klaus-Peter Kiedel of the German Maritime Museum in Bremerhaven, Mrs. Klein of the Photo Archives of Prussian Culture in Berlin, Mr. Koch of the Industry and Trade Office of Hannover-Hildesheim, Herbert Kuke in Bremerhaven, Hero Lang in Bremerhaven, Erika Lisson of the Hapag-Lloyd AG in Bremen, Dr. Mauter of the Markish Museum in Berlin, Jochen W. Meyn of Hamburg-Süd in Hamburg, Dr. Möser in Mannheim, Rolf Müller, proprietor of "Das Topographikon" Publishers in Hamburg, Andrea Peiser of the City Archives in Cuxhaven, Edith Pfeiffer of Hamburg-Süd in Hamburg, Ronald Piechulek of the Rostock Maritime Museum, Dr. Carsten Prange of the museum of Hamburg History, Jens Quedens on the Isle of Amrum, Jana Reid of Hamburg-South in Hamburg, Mrs. Riemer of the Süddeutsche Verlag in Munich, Dr. Volker Rodekamp of the Minden Museum, Dr. Berthold Roland of the Middle Rhenish State Museum in Mainz, Dr. Rolle in Bremen, Dr. Richard Schaffer of the Passau City Museum, Inge-Lore Schlag of the Rostock Maritime Museum, Mr. Schmalfuss of the Museum of Transit and Technology in Berlin, Mrs. Schönemann and Mr. Seeburg of the Cuxhaven City Archives, Gerhard E. Simonsen of the Hapag-Lloyd AG in Hamburg, D. Soltau of the TT Line in Hamburg, Herbert Studtrucker of the German Museum on Munich, Mr. Teichler of KG Ocean Tourism in Flensburg, Mr. Thees of the Cuxhaven City Archives, Erika Weber of the Berliner Verlag photo archives, Mr. Weber of the Ullstein Photo Service in Berlin, Dr. Wechenfelder of the Middle Rhenish Museum in Koblenz, Dr. Kurt Wettengl of the Frankfurt Historical Museum, and of Rita Winkler from the Museum of Hamburg History. Above all, though, thanks are extended to the recently deceased Director of the Focke Museum of Bremen, Dr. Rosemarie Pohl-Weber, Director Gert Schlechtriem and Librarian Arnold Kludas of the German Maritime Museum in Bremerhaven, all three of them closely associated with the publishers and me through long years of mutual interest and cooperation, as well as my American publisher Peter B. Schiffer, who is publishing the English-language edition of this book.

It is also fitting here to remember two great groups of people who are, naturally, not amply depicted in the pictures of the individual ships, but without whom passenger shipping in its historical extent would not have existed. One of these groups is the emigrants. Both the Hapag and the North German Lloyd, the most significant German passenger shipping companies, were founded for the purpose of carrying emigrants to North America, and the profits brought in by these hundreds of thousands of people who traveled across the Atlantic Ocean between decks were what made the grandiose luxury in the first-class accommodations of the ocean giants possible in the first place. When emigration practically came to a stop in the twenties, the passenger ships that were not taken out of service, or used to carry freight as well thanks to their large holds, had to earn their keep primarily from cruises, while the luxury ships, most of them already showing a loss, could be kept running as prestige ships only with governmental support.

The other, the crews of the ships. The *Vaterland*, for example, had a 1234-man crew, and the least of them were seamen. Hundreds served the first- and second-class passengers in kitchen and other services, hundreds worked as stokers and coal trimmers until oil-fired propulsion was introduced between the World Wars. The famous "rushing reporter" Egon Erwin Kisch perceptively said of them aboard the *Vaterland* on June 2, 1914:

"We are standing fifty-five meters below the top of the funnel, aft in Boiler Room No. 4. This 'room' has two wide main streets, each thirty meters long, and four narrow side alleys, each twenty-five meters long, and thus is not a room but a part of a city. Twelve skyscrapers: the boilers. Their fronts are turned toward the two broad avenues, and from here three mighty gates lead into each building, called "fire holes" in the simple language of the technician. There are four boiler rooms; only that nearest the bow has not twelve but only ten of these boilers. Forty-six boilers, as high as houses, with three times forty-six hungry mouths. Two hundred meters long the path measures from the beginning to the end of this massive area of coal, steel, dust, soot and fire.

"There is no rest at night. While still in harbor, the immeasurably vast outside bunkers were filled, a whole mine sank in, thundering, eight thousand, three hundred sixty-four tons as well as an emergency reserve of four hundred ninety-one tons — the coal elevators took twenty hours to load it. Then tending the boilers began for two hundred stokers and two hundred trimmers, the work of turning their own workplace into a landscape of hell. The black stones plunge down from the bunkers in steel wheelbarrows that now swing,

loaded, between the boilers. Then on to the fires. The bell rings. That is the growling of the stomach, the sign of feeding, the music here. Gangs of naked stokers dig into the coals with their shovels and fling the coal between the jaws of the hungry beast. In both lower boilers, in the pipes and soon in the upper boilers too, the water boils, steam rises up, and one hears how it turns the spokes of the wheels up in the machine rooms, how the turbines, the four shafts and the four screws begin to breathe, to live and to throb with the force of sixty thousand horsepower.

The figures by the boilers are black, black like everything else down here. Only when the iron jaws of the boiler open hungrily for a new meal, when the stoker smooths the fire over the grille with an implement four meters long, or when he breaks up the cinders and cleans out the ashes every four hours, does a red light fall on his brow, only then does one see white lines around his eyes and the corners of his mouth, and recognize that this coal formation is a human being.

"The stoker stands and works endlessly, shoving new and newer fodder to the insatiable beast of prey. After four hours, the firemen may leave the arena, relieved by the other shift. Four hours later it all starts again. Like a six-day race. The crossing, too, lasts for six days."

That is what happened down below in the belly of the *Vaterland* and the *Imperator*, shown at the right, the two biggest flagships that ever traveled under the German flag.

Clas Broder Hansen
Isle of Amrum, November 1990

The first modern means of transportation in the age of industry was not the railroad but the steamship, and at first it did not travel the oceans, but linked cities and towns that were situated on rivers. By the end of the 18th Century, there had already been more or less successful test runs of steam-powered ships in Europe and America, and regular steamships service to carry passengers was first established by Robert Fulton in 1807. His paddle steamer *Clermont*, equipped with an engine made by the British firm of Boulton, Watt & Co., ran on the Hudson from New York to Albany. In August of 1812 Henry Bell established the first European steamship line with the *Comet*, running on the Clyde between Glasgow and Greenock.

Shipping with engine-powered craft on German waters began in 1816. On June 11 the British steamer *The Defiance*, coming from Rotterdam, visited the city of Cologne. After a short trip up the Rhine, *The Defiance* passed by Cologne again on its return trip to Rotterdam.

The first German passenger ship was *The Lady Of The Lake*. This wooden paddle steamer, 19.8 meters long, was built in Scotland in 1814 and owned by Peter Kincaid of Glasgow, to whom the senate of Hamburg, on March 6, 1816, granted the exclusive privilege of running steamships between Hamburg and Cuxhaven for four years, and who thereupon became a citizen of Hamburg. No picture of *The Lady Of*

The Lake is known, but it can be assumed that she flew the flag of Hamburg. The ship made its first run from Hamburg to Cuxhaven on June 29, 1816, but regular service turned out to be unprofitable and was given up a year later. *The Lady Of The Lake* returned to Britain.

The water color by F.A. Calau, owned by the Markish Museum in Berlin and shown at the upper right, shows the *Prinzessin Charlotte von Preussen* at the bank of the Spree in front of Bellevue Castle. This ship, named after the eldest daughter of King Friedrich Wilhelm III of Prussia, was the first steamship built in Germany. The Englishman John Barnett Humphreys, who grew up in Germany and was educated in Britain, and his father John Humphreys received, on October 12, 1815, a "patent for the conducting of river shipping with steamships and the permission to run steamships and pass through locks free of tolls" for the whole country of Prussia. On the banks of the Havel in Pichelsdorf near Spandau, now a part of Berlin, J.B. Humphreys set up a "steamship building place", and there on June 29, 1816 the keel was laid; the *Prinzessin Charlotte von Preussen* was launched on September 14. The fourteen-horsepower steam engine, like that of Fulton's *Clermont*, was obtained from Boulton, Watt & Co. of Soho near Birmingham, then England's most important machine factory. With a deck length of some 41 meters and a beam of six meters, the

Prinzessin Charlotte was a ship of some size. She was built of wood and driven by a central wheel 3.35 meters in diameter, whose wheelhouse rose well above the deck and also included the entrance to the forward salon. To bring the water needed for forward motion to the paddle wheel, a sort of tunnel was built into the entire length of the ship's bottom, its top remaining above water level even at maximum draught of barely 60 centimeters. Thus the ship was a sort of double-hulled craft below, had two keels, but only one stem and one sternpost. Forward as well as aft, there was a large, elegantly appointed "Cajüte" and a smaller "Cabinett" below decks. Up to 300 passengers could be carried.

After several test runs, the *Prinzessin Charlotte von Preussen* made her first run on October 27, 1816, carrying 160 invited guests to Peacock Island, and on November 2 His Majesty, the King of Prussia became the first monarch ever to ride on a steamship. Line service with paying passengers began on November 5, running from Berlin-Tiergarten to Charlottenburg, and often also to Spandau and Potsdam.

In the following years, Humphreys built four more steamers in Pichelsdorf and later in Potsdam, all equipped with machinery from Boulton, Watt & Co. The second steamship built in Germany, the *Kurier*, also called *Der Kurier* or *Courier*, was launched at Pichelsdorf on March 15, 1817. She was a side-wheel steamer, 40 meters long. Her first voyage, beginning on April 5,

followed the Havel and Elbe rivers to Hamburg, where the ship arrived with passengers and freight on April 8. The *Kurier* was the first steamship to make the run between Berlin and Hamburg. The *Friedrich Wilhelm III*, built in 1818, also made numerous runs to Hamburg with passengers, while the *Stadt Magdeburg*, built in 1817, and the *Fürst Blücher* of 1819 were used only for freight and towing.

Humphreys' first German shipping company was not destined to be successful. As early as 1821 he gave up the business, had the machinery removed from the ships, and auctioned off their hulls in 1824 and 1825.

The paddle steamer *Die Weser*, shown in a water-color drawing of 1819, was launched even before the *Kurier* of Berlin, on December 30, 1816, but took up line service only on May 20, 1817, running from Bremen via Vegesack to Brake, where the large sailing ships of the Bremen shipping lines anchored on account of the silting of the Weser. Thus she was the third steamship built in Germany. *Die Weser*, measuring some 25 meters in length and likewise driven by a machine made by the British firm of Boulton, Watt & Co., was contracted for by the Bremen merchant Friedrich Schröder and built as number 30 at the shipyard of Johann Lange in Grohn, near Vegesack. Until 1833 she ran between Bremen and Brake, as well as to Bremerhaven after the city was founded in 1827.

The *Herzog von Cambridge* depicted below her, built for Friedrich Schröder by Jürgen Sager in Vegesack, was put into service in Ocotber of 1818 and was the first steamer on the upper Weser, though she ran primarily, like the *Weser*, from Bremen to Vegesack. From 1820 to 1831 she was used only for towing and carried no more passengers.

The Hollanders were the first to set up a regular steamship service on the Rhine, in 1822. The Nederlandsche Stoomboot Maatschappij extended its line to Cologne in 1824 and ran the ships *De Zeeuw*, *James Watt* and *De Rijn*. In 1826 the Preussisch-Rheinische Dampfschiffahrtgesellschaft was founded, and on May 1, 1827 the first German Rhine steamer, the *Concordia* shown at the lower left, was put into service between Cologne and Mainz. The *Concordia* had been built in The Netherlands. Her wooden hull was 42.7 meters long, the British steam engine produced 70 horsepower

and turned the paddle wheels at a rate of thirty revolutions per minute, moving the ship with its 230 passengers upstream at 10.5 kilometers per hour. At the end of May 1827 the *Friedrich Wilhelm,* an identical sister ship to the *Concordia,* was put into service, likewise running regularly between Cologne and Mainz. Both ships were sold to Rotterdam in 1840.

In the oil painting by Lorenz Petersen above, the *Neptun* is seen on the Köhlbrand steaming past flat Elbe islands on its way toward the Harburg Hills. Hamburg and nearby Harburg, which belonged to Hannover, were thus linked by water, as there was no bridge over the Elbe then, and one of the first German steamship lines was opened between the two cities by Peter Kleudgen on June 14, 1818. The Harburger Dampffähre, a steamer with central wheel like the *Prinzessin Charlotte von Preussen,* ran on this route until October of 1829 and was replaced the following month by the *Neptun* shown above. This steamer, some 33 meters long, was ordered from Johann Lange at Grohn near Vegesack by Peter Kleudgen's widow and launched there, as number 85, on September 5, 1829. The *Neptun* could carry 400 passengers as well as coaches. On October 1, 1841 she was replaced by the iron steamer *Alexandrine,* which was renamed *Phönix* in 1843.

On the Bodensee, the shippers' guilds feared for their traditional rights and tried to prevent competition from steamships, as was done on other waters as well. King Wilhelm I of Württemberg bought the shippers' rights from them and turned them over to the newly founded state-owned Friedrichshafener Dampfbootgesellschaft. This firm had a ship built that measured 30.6 meters long, with a beam of 5.4 meters and 10.8 meters over its wheelhouses; it was launched under the name of *Wilhelm* on August 17, 1824 and fitted with a 21-horsepower engine made by the Liverpool firm of Fawcett. As of December 1, 1824 this first Bodensee steamship made four trips a week, with up to 124 passengers and mail, from Friedrichshafen to Rorschach in Switzerland, but also made pleasure cruises and carried freight to other towns. The picture below shows the *Wilhelm* off Friedrichshafen.

Only two days after the *Wilhelm*, the 22.8-meter steamer *Max Joseph* went into service, based at Lindau in Bavaria and owned by Consul Church and Baron von Cotta; she usually ran out of ports in Baden such as Konstanz, but also regularly from Lindau via Rorschach to Schaffhausen.

Above: On the night of August 7-8, 1844 a fire, presumably set by arsonists, destroyed the *Kronprinz von Hannover* at the pier in her home port of Harburg. The first steamship under the flag of Hannover, she was put into service on May 1, 1839 by a consortium of Harburg shipowners and served the route between Harburg and Hamburg since then. The builder of the 42-meter wooden hull was Johann Beenck of Altona, and the steam engine was made by Georg Egestorff of Linden near Hannover, whose price was 30% lower than those of the British bidders. After 1844, only iron steamers ran between Hamburg and Harburg.

Right: The 35-meter wooden steamer *Elbe*, built at Port Glasgow in 1833 for the Hamburger Dampfschiffahrts-Compagnie, was Germany's first sea resort ship. Normally running between Hamburg and Cuxhaven, it went on to Helgoland on summer weekends, first reaching there on June 21, 1834, or to Norderney or Wyk on Föhr. In 1836 a second ship of this firm, the somewhat larger *Patriot*, took up the same resort service.

Above: The *Königin Maria* was Saxony's first steamer, and one of the Continent's first iron ships. The 36-meter hull was built in Dresden, the machinery in Berlin. After being put into service in the summer of 1837 by the Elbdampfschiffahrts-Gesellschaft, which had been granted a privileged status by the Saxon government, she ran up the Elbe from Dresden to Schandau and Tetschen, downstream to Meissen and beyond. She was scrapped in 1846.

Lower left: The *Eduard,* built of fir wood by the ship's carpenter Heinrich Hagemann at Hannoversch Münden in 1843 and measuring 29 meters long over her deck, was the first steamer to run up the Fulda to Kassel. Most of the time, though, the *Eduard* was used on the upper Weser between Münden and Hameln. The cabin for 24 first-class passengers, "elegantly decorated, tastefully painted, with a semicircular Ottoman of red velvet plush" was located forward, the cabin for a like number of second-class passengers was aft.

In the first decades, steamship commerce had to deal with the most varied difficulties. Engineering technology and machine technology were just in their infancy, and thus it often happened that the ships could not attain the speeds calculated by their designers and thus could make fewer voyages per year, or even could scarcely run upstream. At rapids or sharp bends in the rivers, horses were usually used for towing on upstream trips in any case. The heavy low-pressure machines originally used gave the steamers a much greater draught than had been planned, so that they often grounded. The rivers were not yet regulated or canalized, and the removal of shallows through dredging began gradually only in the forties of the 19th Century. For example, the draught of the *Königin Maria*, shown at the upper left, was only 80 centimeters when fully laden and carrying 300 passengers, but this was much too great, so that the ship frequently ran aground and had to be tied up when the Elbe was low.

The unreliability of the early steam engines often necessitated long, laborious repairs. These technical problems, not to mention the lack of commercial experience in the use of machine-powered vehicles, led to the great majority of the new steamship lines founded in the 1830s being financial failures.

Nonetheless, the introduction of steamship traffic, even in its very first years, still represented tremendous progress in travel. The steamships were generally even faster, and in any case certainly more comfortable, than the fastest horse-drawn mail coaches. Even before the day of the steamer, people usually traveled downstream by boat, with the trip from Mainz to Koblenz. for example, taking one full day. But the steamer only needed four and a half hours for the same trip.

Upstream, when the boats had to be towed, water travel was very time-consuming and thus scarcely practical. The steamships, on the other hand, needed scarcely more time for the trip upstream than the trip downstream had previously taken.

On rivers where large numbers of passengers were at hand, such as the Rhine, where the old privileges of river towns and shipping guilds were gradually lifted, as were the monopolies granted to the first steamship companies, several firms were already competing with each other, offering the traveler an ever-greater frequency of departures. By the end of the thirties, steamship lines had already been established on all of Germany's major waterways.

In the 1851 woodcut shown below, the Main steamer *Königin Marie*, built in the yards of the Maindampf-schiffahrtsgesellschaft in Würzburg, passes the city of Würzburg.

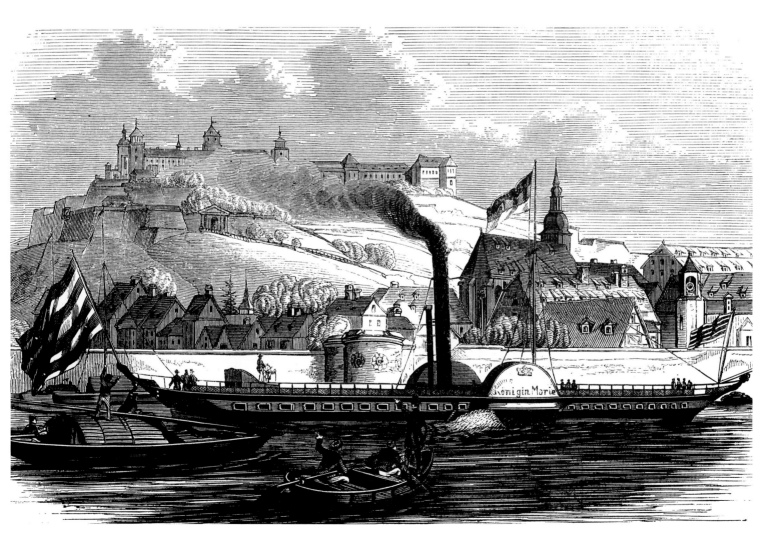

In the forties, though, competition for the steamboats appeared in the form of a new means of transportation, the railroad. Thus the railroad line built from Cologne to Bonn in 1844 and extended to Koblenz in 1858 immediately caused a very decisive decrease in the importance of steamship travel on that line. But since the construction of a gapless network of railway lines took decades, the era of more than thirty years in which the steamship was the fastest and most important means of transporting passengers inland came to an end only gradually. Despite the railroad, though, the number of steamers, which were now used more and more

for excursions on rivers and lakes too, continued to increase in that time of rapidly increasing mobility.

After the first iron ship, built in Britain and intended for transportation on the Seine, had gone into service in 1821, iron ships also appeared in Germany in the thirties. The first iron ship built in Germany, the *Prinz Karl,* was built at Berlin-Moabit in 1835; the second was the *Königin Maria''* (see page 14). The Gutehoffnung Iron Works in Ruhrort built the first two iron Rhine steamers, the *Graf von Paris* and the 4ST2Stadt Mannheim, in 1838 and 1839. The first iron ship based in Hamburg was the *Primus,* built at Blackwall near

London in 1839.

The first iron ship on the Weser was the paddle steamer *Telegraph,* shown below passing the city of Bremen in a painting by Carl Justus Harmen Fedeler. Ordered by six Bremen merchants, she was built at Millwall near London by Wm. Fairbairn & Co. in the spring of 1840. The *Telegraph* was barely 40 meters long, ran at nine knots and could carry up to 350 passengers. She was put into sea-resort service from Bremen to Wangerooge and Norderney. In 1872 she was sold and broken up.

In the first 25 years of German steamship travel, the ships had run only on rivers and lakes, plus to Helgoland and the North Frisian Islands. The steam engines worked too ineffectively at first, the amount of coal to be taken along would have been too great for a voyage over a longer stretch of ocean to have been practical. Only in the early forties, from Hamburg as of 1841 and Bremen as of 1843, did a few steamers run to England and Holland.

In overseas travel the more practical screw propeller was soon established, while paddle wheels still prevailed for a long time on the rivers, since

they had their advantages in narrow, shallow waters. The first German screw steamers were the *Horsa* and *Hengist*, built of iron in Britain, which ran between Brake and the English port of Hull as of 1845.

Hamburg's first propeller-driven ships were the *Hammonia*, launched in 1846, and her sister ship, the *Archimedes*, which was put into service ten months later and is depicted in the painting by Lorenz Petersen shown above. She probably got her name from the famous British *Archimedes* of 1839, the world's first seagoing screw steamer. The Hamburg *Archimedes*, an iron

steamer some 40 meters long, was built in 1846 in the T.D. Marshall shipyards at South Sjields, in northern England, and delivered to the Elbe-Humber Dampfschiffahrt Gesellschaft, which was founded in the same year and ran the ship on 18 to 24 round voyages from Hamburg to Hull with freight and passengers. In 1858 she was sold to the firm of H.J. Perlbach in Hamburg. At first the *Archimedes* continued to run to Hull, but as of 1861 generally to Antwerp and Holland, where she ran aground in March of 1864.

Upper left: This early photo shows the *Maximilian*, the first steamship on the Starnberger See. The 33.5-meter iron hull and the wood-fired engine were produced by the Maffai locomotive factory in Munich. The ship was assembled at Starnberg and launched there on March 11, 1851 in the presence of King Maximilian II of Bavaria. The drawings for the figurehead and the carved decorations of the interior were made by the Munich Academy director Wilhelm von Kaulbach. Until 1885 the *Maximilian* covered the whole length of the Starnberger See from Starnberg to

Seeshaupt; then she was dismantled and transported to the Ammersee in pieces, on which she was used until being scrapped in 1895.

Left: Typical ocean steamships of the fifties were the iron screw ships *Erbgrossherzog Friedrich Franz* and *Grossfürst Constantin* of 1857, both rigged as three-masted topsail schooners. They belonged to the Rostock Petersburger Dampfschiffahrts Gesellschaft of Rostock and were used in line service from there to Petrograd. This service had been established in 1852 with two smaller ships bearing the same names, the

first iron steamers built in Rostock.

Above: The first German shipping firm that maintained line service across the Atlantic with several steamships was the Hamburg-America Line (see page 24), which began in 1856. The contemporary lithograph shows the whole Hapag fleet at the end of 1858; from left to right, the *Saxonia*, the sailing ships *Elbe* and Deutschland, the steamer *Hammonia*, in front of it the tender *Schulau*, then the full-rigged ships *Main, Oder, Donau* and *Neckar* and the steamships *Teutonia, Borussia* and *Bavaria*.

Barely three decades after the first river steamship lines were established, technology had developed to the extent that steamships could also be used in overseas transit. In 1838 the *Sirius* and the *Great Western* were the first to cross the Atlantic under steam power, and in 1840 Samuel Cunard set up a mail steamship line between Liverpool and Boston, with support from the British government, and had four wooden paddle steamers, the *Britannia*, *Acadia* (the later German *Germania*), *Caldeonia* and *Columbia* built in Scotland. As of 1845 the iron screw steamer *Great Britain*, built by the renowned Isambard Kingdom Brunel and gigantic and highly modern for those times, provided

Atlantic service. The first steamship line running between America and a German port landed at Bremerhaven. Here the *Washington* was in service as of 1847 and the *Hermann* as of 1848; both were wooden paddle steamers flying the American flag.

The first German transatlantic steamer, though, was the *Helena Sloman*. Robert M. Sloman, proprietor of the largest Hamburg sailing-ship company, who had established the first German steamship route to Britain in 1841, had this relatively small but modern iron screw steamer built in Hull, England. The *Helena Sloman*, built to carry 42 first-class, 32 second-class and 236 steerage passengers, left her

home port of Hamburg on May 29, 1850 under Captain Paul Nickels of Föhr and reached New York on June 29. Her return trip took only eighteen days. But on her third voyage, in November of 1850, she encountered a heavy storm on the North Atlantic, and after a nine-day battle the leaking ship had to be abandoned. All but nine of the passengers and crew were picked up by a British sailing ship.

The water-color below by J. Gottheil, owned by the firm of Robert M. Sloman, Jr. shows the *Helena Sloman* on the Elbe before her first departure, with St. Michael's Church and the Harbor Gate of Hamburg in the background.

The second German shipping firm to use steamships for their North Atlantic service was the Bremen firm of W.A. Fritze & Co. This company had bought two paddle steamers of the first German navy, which had been auctioned off in 1853, the *Erzherzog Johann*, built in 1840 as the passenger ship *Acadia* and now renamed *Germania*, and the *Hansa*, shown above, already flying the Fritze house flag, in a water-color owned by the Maritime Museum in Brake; it had been launched in New York in 1847 as the passenger ship *United States*. The *Hansa* displaced 1857 tons, measured 74 meters long over the deck and could carry 50 first-class and 700 steerage passengers. The *Hansa* and the 1135-ton *Germania* ran between Bremerhaven and New York as of August 1853, were chartered by the British government for use as troop transports in the Crimean War in 1855, and sold in Britain in 1857 and 1858, as they had proved to be unprofitable. They were the only wooden German ocean liners.

The early transatlantic steamers still resembled sailing ships very much both above and below decks until the end of the seventies. They had a clear full-length upper deck without superstructures except a wheelhouse and small deck houses. As on sailing ships, the first cabin, as the first-class accommodations were then called, were aft in the last third of the hull, and on the main deck, the highest full-length and fully enclosed deck, just under the upper deck. The second cabin was usually amidships at both sides of the engine and funnel shaft, and the crew's quarters were forward. Underneath was the steerage or between-decks, so called because in these early ships it was the only deck between the main deck and the hold. The steerage was only used for passengers on the westward voyage; on the way back it was used to carry freight.

The first-class cabins formed a long row on each side of the ship, and each one had a porthole. From the cabins one stepped directly into the long, narrow salon that lay between them, its light coming only from above via skylights. The space was barely more than two meters high and was used not only as a dining hall but as a sitting room too. In the center was a long row of tables. The benches usually had folding backs, so that the passengers could sit with their backs to the table when they were not eating meals.

The picture at upper left shows passengers playing chess in the first-class salon of the Norddeutsche Lloyd's fifth transatlantic steamer, the *Hansa*, built in 1861; the photo at lower left shows the deck of one of the first Hapag steamers, probably the *Saxonia* of 1857, while docked at New York around 1860.

Upper right: The first Lloyd steamer, the *Adler* (664 tons, length 54 meters over the bow, 46 passengers), went into service on October 1, 1857. She was built not for transatlantic service, but ran to London and Hull in England, a service that the Lloyd maintained until 1897, usually with six ships.

In 1847, Hamburg merchants founded the Hamburg-Amerikanische Paketfahrt-Actien-Gesellschaft, HAPAG for short, later also called the Hamburg-America Line, using sailing ships to provide line service, primarily for emigrants to America. In 1854 the stockholders decided to acquire large modern steamers to offer regular service from Hamburg to New York every two weeks.

The first of these ships, the *Hammonia*, displacing 2026 tons and measuring 85 meters at the waterline, was launched on May 5, 1855, and her sister ship *Borussia* followed two months later. They were built by the Scottish shipyards of Caird & Co. in Greenock on the Clyde, which provided almost all the Hapag steamers and most of the Lloyd's for two decades. *Hammonia* and *Borussia*

were iron screw steamers which, powered by 1400-HP oscillating steam engines, had a top speed of eleven knots. They had accommodations for 54 first-class and 146 second-class passengers, plus 310 emigrants in steerage.

Hammonia and *Borussia* did not go into transatlantic service as soon as they were delivered, but were chartered by the French and British governments for use as troop transports during the Crimean War. On June 1, 1856 the *Borussia* then became the first Hapag steamer to begin line service from Hamburg to New York, with the *Hammonia* following a month later.

In 1857 the Hapag put two more steamers, weighing some 600 tons and measuring ten meters longer, into service, the *Austria* and *Saxonia*.

On September 13, 1858 the woodwork of the *Austria* caught fire on the Atlantic when the steerage was being disinfected by smoke, and the ship burned and sank. This was the worst steamer loss to date, as 449 persons lost their lives, only 89 being rescued. To replace the *Austria*, the Hapag obtained the *Teutonia* and the *Petropolis* (see page 29), which was renamed *Bavaria*, from a competitor, the Hamburg-Brasilischen Dampfschiffahrt-Gesellschaft. At the end of 1858 the Hapag had five steamships in North Atlantic service (see page 19).

The painting shown above, from the Museum of Hamburg History, shows the *Borussia*, with the *Hammonia* in the left background.

The Hapag faced competition on the Atlantic as early as 1858 from the Norddeutsche Lloyd of Bremen, founded a year before, which offered line service from Bremerhaven to New York with four iron screw steamers.

The Lloyd's first transatlantic steamer was the *Bremen*, depicted below in a painting by Fritz Müller now in the Focke Museum. She was launched at Cairds of Greenock on February 1, 1858, displaced 2674 tons, was 101 meters long overall, and had a capacity of 60 first-class, 110 second-class and 400 steerage passengers. On June 19, 1858 the *Bremen*, under Captain Heinrich Wessels, left Bremerhaven for the first time. On board were 22 cabin and 93 steerage passengers, plus 150 tons of freight and mail. On the morning of July 4, after a voyage of 14 days and 13 hours, she arrived in New York.

Her sister ship, the *New York*, was likewise built by Cairds, the somewhat smaller two-funnel steamers *Hudson* and *Weser* at Palmers in Yarrow. All three ships went into service in 1858. The *Hudson* (see page 23) was burned out at Bremerhaven in the same year, the *Weser* was sold in 1859 after being damaged in a storm, while the *Bremen* and *New York* ran under the Norddeutsche Lloyd flag until 1874.

The first railroad ferry on the Continent of Europe — aside from short river crossings — was established on the Bodensee between Friedrichshafen and Romanshorn. The first train ferry, shown above, was built in Friedrichshafen, Württemberg by the Swiss firm of Escher & Wyss to plans by John Scott Russel, the builder of the *Great Eastern*. It belonged to the Royal Württemberg State Railways, but the Swiss Railway Company had also contributed to paying for it. The

steam ferry, which had no name, went into service in 1869 and ran until 1885. Measuring 70 meters in length, she was the biggest ship ever to run on the Bodensee.

Upper right: The overseas steamers, once they had loaded their freight, often left the harbor and lay at anchor in the Elbe or Weser. Shortly before the voyage began, the passengers and their luggage were ferried to them on passenger boats known as tenders. The woodcut made in 1871 by Carl

Fedeler shows the tender *Lloyd* of the Norddeutsche Lloyd on the Weser off Bremerhaven.

Lower right: In front of the Lloyd Hall, built at the New Harbor in Bremerhaven in 1869, emigrants are transferring from the train to the *Rhein*, built in 1868. Before the railroad line was built in 1861, the passengers had to travel down the Weser from Bremen to Bremerhaven in open lighters on tow.

Shown at left is the sea resort steamer *Helgoland,* built by Cairds in Greenock; she was the first iron ship on the Helgoland run. Johann César Godeffroy & Son of Hamburg put the steamer into service in July of 1854. The *Helgoland* attained a speed of 15 knots and took some seven hours for the voyage from Hamburg to Helgoland, only half as long as the old wooden steamers *Elbe* and *Patriot* (see page 13). She was sold in England in 1863.

Lower left: The *Hermann* of 1865 (2713 tons) was the Nordeeutsche Lloyd's seventh transatlantic steamer.

The painting below shows the *Petropolis* of the Hamburg-Brasilische Dampfschiffahrt-Gesellschaft, a firm founded by Hamburg business houses in 1855 for the South American trade. The firm had two iron screw steamers built by Cairds of Greenock; each was 90 meters long at the waterline and could carry 500 passengers, 310 of them in steerage.

The *Teutonia* made its first voyage to Brazil in 1856, the 2405-ton *Petrololis* in 1857.

The firm soon got into financial difficulties and had to declare bankruptcy in 1858. The *Teutonia* and the *Petropolis,* which was renamed *Bavaria,* were taken over by the Hapag (see page 24).

From 1873 to 1875 a classic capitalistic competition took place in German passenger shipping. The Deutsche Transatlantische Dampfschiffahrts-Gesellschaft of Hamburg, usually called the Adler Line after the firm's eagle emblem, was founded in 1872 in the boom of the "founding years", in part with inland capital, and contracted with various Glasgow shipyards for eight passenger ships that, displacing some 3500 tons each, were bigger than the Hapag and Lloyd steamers. They were also more comfortably furnished, equipped with modern compound engines, and at 13 knots they ran one to two knots faster than the competition. They could carry 990 passengers, 800 of them in steerage.

The first Adler Line ship, the *Goethe,* ran from Hamburg to New York in 1873; in 1874 there followed the *Herder, Schiller, Lessing* and *Klopstock.* In the same year, though, the financial upswing came to an end, and the number of passengers on the North Atlantic route fell off tremendously. The Adler Line did not put their newly-built *Wieland* and *Gellert* into service immediately. Hapag, Lloyd and the Adler Line began to undercut each other in passenger prices again and again, until the steamers could no longer meet their expenses. This ruinous competition plunged all three firms into red ink and could not be kept up for long. The Adler line, burdened by heavy interest charges, had to give up, selling their whole fleet to Hapag in 1875. This line now owned more ships than it could actually use, and for years it did not put any new ships into service.

The photo below shows the *Wieland,* built for the Adler Line in 1874, in Hamburg harbor, with St. Michael's and St. Catherine's church steeples in the background. She is seen here, already under the Hapag flag, after being rebuilt in 1882, which gave her a second funnel and a higher superstructure.

The picture above shows, at right in the drydock, the Lloyd steamer *Hohenstaufen*, built by Earles in Hull and one of the thirteen ships of the 3000-ton *Strasburg* class. At left is one of the typical Norddeutsche Lloyd steamers built by Cairds in Greenock at the end of the sixties, still with a clipper bow but without a bowsprit.

Above: The *Silesia,* built in 1869, and the *Vandalia* of 1871, visible in the left background, belonged to the second *Hammonia* class of the Hapag, with which, as of 1867, German steamers of more than 3000 tons first came into service. The Hapag ships of the sixties, unlike those of the Lloyd, no longer had the clipper bows of the sailing ships, and the number of sail-carrying masts was reduced to two.

Lower left: The Hapag's 3678-ton *Moravia,* which could carry 1200 emigrants, was built by Inglis in Glasgow and ran on the Hamburg-New York route as of 1883. Three years later she opened a new line service from Stettin to New York.

Upper right: The 2438-ton *Buenos Aires,* built in Sunderland, belonged to the Hamburg-Südamerikanischen Dampfschiffahrt-Gesellschaft, founded in 1871 and known as Hamburg-Süd for short, and was the firm's largest ship until 1887; as of 1873 she ran from Hamburg via Lisbon to Bahia, Rio de Janeiro, Santos, Montevideo and Buenos Aires. The first cabin held 30, the steerage 200 passengers, mostly Portuguese and Spanish agricultural workers who traveled to South America for the harvest season.

Lower right: the 2689-ton *Polaria,* built in Newcastle in 1882, carried 1100 passengers in steerage alone and was one of those ships with which, as of 1881, the Hamburg shipowner Edward Carr and his emigrant agent Albert Ballin offered a cheap passage to the ever-growing flood of emigrants, now also coming from Eastern Europe, who sought a new home in America. Soon Carr, Hapag and Lloyd were waging a bitter price war, with prices falling to new lows until the competition finally ended with the price agreement of 1885 and the establishment of a combined service by Hapag and the Union Line, meanwhile founded by Carr and Sloman. Part of the agreement was the employment by Hapag of young Albert Ballin, who first became the director of their passenger department and later their famous director.

After 1880 the Norddeutsche Lloyd began to put eleven high-speed steamers into use on their line service to New York. With them, the firm first equaled the international standard for passenger shipping. Nine units of this so-called River Class were built in Glasgow by John Elder and his successor form of Fairfield.

It began in 1881 with the *Elbe*, the first German high-speed steamer. In 1882 came the *Werra*, shown at upper left. She displaced 4815 tons, was 131 meters long at the waterline, reached a cruising speed of 16 knots with her 6000-HP compound engine, and could carry 190 first-class, 144 second-class and 868 steerage passengers. Further ships of this type were the *Fulda* of 1883, the *Eider* and the *Ems*, shown at left center, of 1884.

In 1886, somewhat larger ships, the *Aller*, *Trave* and *Saale*, came into service, no longer built of iron but rather of steel, the first high-speed steamers in the world to be equipped with the more effectively working triple-expansion engines and attain a speed of 17 knots. The *Lahn* of 1887 was even one knot faster.

The Lloyd could now offer three departures a week from Bremerhaven to New York and carried more passengers across the Atlantic than any other line. But the River Class steamers, with their 5000-ton displacement and single screw propellers, followed an outmoded concept, as twin-screw steamers displacing over 10,000 tons were already crossing the Atlantic at over 20 knots.

The *Spree* and the *Havel* (shown on page 56), the last two ships of the River Class and the first built at a German shipyard, the Vulcan in Stettin, seemed a bit anachronistic when they were put into service in 1890 and 1891. Thus the *Spree* was converted to twin-screw drive in 1900. The picture at lower left shows her, now renamed *Kaiserin Maria Theresia*, after the rebuilding which lengthened her by twenty meters and gave her a third funnel.

Upper right: The *Darmstadt* embarks from Wilhelmshaven on August 31, 1900 with troops of the Expeditionary Corps sent to China

because of the Boxer Rebellion. She was one of six 5300-ton Lloyd steamers built in Glasgow between 1889 and 1891 that combined moderate 13-knot speeds, high freight capacity and steerage accommodations for almost 2000 passengers, and were used alternately on all the firm's lines.

The picture at right does not show the *Gera*, as the retouched lettering suggests, but the *Karlsruhe*, built in 1889 and a sister ship to the *Gera* and *Darmstadt*.

Left: The *Fürst Bismarck*, placed in service in 1891, was the fourth and, at 8874 tons, the largest high-speed steamer of the *Augusta Victoria* Class; here she is leaving Cuxhaven on her way to New York.

Top: The 7661-ton *Augusta Victoria*, 145 meters long overall, was the first high-speed Hapag steamer; here she passes Stadersand on her way up the Elbe.

Above: The *Normannia*, built in 1890 by Fairfields in Glasgow and displacing 8716 tons, accommodated 420 first-class, 172 second-class and 700 steerage passengers, as did the *Fürst Bismarck*.

With these new steamers, the Hapag moved into the top group of international passenger-ship companies. The *Augusta Victoria* was innovative in two ways: she was the third high-

speed steamer in the world with twin screws and the first to be built at a German shipyard, the Vulcan of Stettin. The firm's decision to contract in Germany for a ship that was to attain the highest technical standards of the time was then not only unusual but downright brave.

Two months after the *Augusta Victoria*, the *Columbia*, built by Lairds of Birkenhead, went into service. Both achieved a cruising speed of 18 knots and could reach a top speed of 19.5 knots. The high-speed steamer service proved to be so successful that it was planned to expand it to a weekly tempo soon. For this purpose the *Normannia* was built in Scotland in 1890, and the *Fürst Bismarck* was built by Vulcan of Stettin and put into service in 1891. They were a good 1000 tons heavier, 15 meters longer and more than one knot faster than their forerunners.

The Hapag high-speed steamers were neither the biggest nor the fastest ships on the North Atlantic. In terms of speed, they were beaten by about one knot by the newest steamers of the leading British lines. These, though, traveled the main route on the Atlantic between Liverpool and New York, and thus were not in direct competition with the German lines. But on the Channel route via Southampton, also served by the Belgians, Hollanders and particularly the French, the Hapag steamers led in every sense.

In 1897 the *Augusta Victoria* was rebuilt, lengthened, and renamed *Auguste Victoria*. The *Normannia* was sold to the Spanish in 1898, the other three steamers to the Russians in 1904.

By now the ocean liner had nothing in common with the earlier steamers in terms of interior decor. The British *Oceanic* in 1870 and the Lloyd River Class, for the first time in Germany, no longer had their first-class cabins at the stern, but was moved to amidships on an additional upper deck. The complete elimination of sails, which gradually went out of use with the introduction of dependable twin-screw steamers as of the late eighties, was a prerequisite for ever-roomier passenger accommodations in several upper decks.

The Hapag high-speed steamers of the *Augusta Victoria* Class already had social rooms on two complete upper decks, decorated in a pompous neo-rococo style. The first-class dining room had now risen to the superstructure of the upper deck, but was still only one deck high and had in its center the customary light shaft, the so-called "cathedral", that cut through the deck above. On the bridge deck there were first-class suites as well as ladies' and music salons.

The picture at left shows the first-class dining room of the *Fürst Bismarck* with its "cathedral" rising in the center' that below shows the ladies' salon of the *Columbia*.

To promote trade with Germany's newly-acquired colonies and improve the German export trade, the Reichstag decided in 1885 to establish mail steamship lines to East Asia and Australia and support them with subsidies. It was required that the new steamers had to be built at German shipyards. This regulation contributed greatly to cooperation between the German shipbuilding industry and the British shipyards in the coming years.

The concession to provide Imperial postal service went to the Norddeutsche Lloyd, which began by ordering three large and three smaller steamers from the Vulcan yards of Stettin. The first mail steamer to go into service was the *Preussen* in 1886; it displaced 4577 tons, ran at 14 knots and could carry, besides freight, 100 first-class, 28 second-class and 202 steerage passengers.

The picture below shows the *Preussen* after being rebuilt in 1894 by Blohm & Voss; the ship was lengthened in drydock and the funnels were raised. The Lloyd's Imperial mail steamers were the first to have their funnels painted a yellow ochre color.

In the 19th Century the emigrants were the vital source of profit for the passenger-ship lines and the main reason for the growth of overseas traffic and the ships' size. British lines transported chiefly the masses of Irish leaving their country for America, while the German lines carried emigrants going overseas from the German lands, and profited increasingly from the ever-growing numbers of emigrants from eastern

European countries since the eighties.

Not only the famous high-speed steamers, on which the first-class accommodations became more and more opulent and gained more and more space and importance, carried these emigrants, but so did great numbers of unspectacular ships that looked rather like freighters and were used as such on the return trips, after the steerage accommodations were dismantled. These ships traveled considerably more slowly than the high-speed luxury liners but offered a lower-priced crossing and had the decisive advantage of carrying no, or almost no, cabin passengers, and thus the entire deck area could be used to carry steerage passengers.

A typical representative of this type of ship was the 2889-ton *Christiania*, shown above with emigrants, of which she could carry 620, on deck and running from Antwerp to America. She was built in 1890 by Blohm & Voss for the Dampfschiff-Reederei Hansa of Hamburg, which was later taken over by the Hapag. The *Baumwall* came under the Hapag flag in 1894 and was renamed *Christiania* in 1895. After being sold to Stettin owners, she sank off Borkum in 1913.

Left: The 685-ton twin-screw steamer *Prinz Waldemar*, built by the Howaldt Works in Kiel in 1893, was 66 meters long and reached 13 knots; it was first used by the Kiel firm of Sartori & Berger for line service to Swinemünde and Stettin. Later, like its sister ships *Prinz Adalbert* (1895) and *Prinz Sigismund* (1900), it was used on the Kiel-Corsór line, at that time the fastest connection between Hamburg and Copenhagen.

Below: The *Najade* of the Norddeutsche Lloyd, built by Schichau in Danzig, displaced 724 tons, measured 71 meters long and achieved 16 knots; she carried up to 670 passengers from the Weser to Helgoland from 1894 until she was replaced by the *Roland* in 1927.

Lower left: The 804-ton twin-screw steamer *Silvana*, built by Howaldt in Kiel, joined Ballin's Nordsee-Linie in 1897; the line was taken over by the Hapag in 1905. Until World War I the 14-knot ship, built to carry 618 passengers, generally ran between Hamburg and Helgoland, and also to the North Sea resorts of Wyk on Föhr, Wittdün on Amrum and Hörnum on Sylt.

Upper right: The large salon paddle steamer *Cobra*, built by Fairfields of Glasgow for a British customer in 1889 and bought by Ballin's Dampfschiff-Reederei, the later Nordsee-Linie, in 1890. spent three decades in resort service, running from Hamburg and Cuxhaven to Helgoland and Sylt, and in some years to the Riviera during the winter too. The *Cobra* was 85 meters long, displaced 1146 tons, reached 14.5 knots and could carry 912 passengers.

Lower right: The 919-ton *Prinzessin Heinrich*, delivered by Blohm & Voss in 1896, also belonged to Albert Ballin's resort fleet and was taken over by the Hapag in 1905. Carrying up to 540 passengers at 14 knots, she ran down the lower Elbe and to Helgoland until she was wrecked in 1923.

Above: The 5463-ton *Ambria*, built by the Flensburger Schiffsbaugesellschaft, was one of sixteen ships known as the A steamers for their initials. They were put into service by the Hapag between 1896 and 1901 for freight and emigrant service. The *Ambria* could carry 50 cabin and 235 steerage passengers. She went into Hapag service in 1897, but was used only for freight as of 1904.

Below: The *Silvia*, also built in Flensburg in 1901, was also one of the A steamers, not all of which were sister ships, despite her name. Here she is seen leaving Hamburg harbor with emigrants on deck. The 6506-ton *Silvia* was 128 meters long at the water line, made 11 knots and carried 58 cabin and 1038 steerage passengers.

Below: The Hapag's 10,237-ton *Bulgaria*, seen here leaving the harbor of Genoa, was built by Blohm & Voss in 1898 as one of the five big B Class twin-screw steamers. Like the smaller A steamers and the gigantic P steamers (see page 54), they followed a concept that had nothing to do with the high-speed steamer but proved to be economically successful: they were very slow (12 knots) and carried practically no first-class passengers but had an enormous capacity in their holds and steerage. The 157-meter *Bulgaria* could carry six first-class and 264 second-class passengers, but 2333 in steerage. After being rebuilt in 1906, the last number increased to 2741. She ran mainly on the North Atlantic route from Hamburg and Cuxhaven to New York, Boston or Baltimore.

Bottom: In 1898 Blohm & Voss delivered the *Syria*, a newly-built 3597-ton steamer, to the Hapag for line service to the West Indies. She had a registered length of 105 meters, accommodations for 32 first-class and 88 — later almost 600 — steerage passengers, and made 11 knots.

45

In 1894 the Norddeutsche Lloyd put two new twin-screw steamers into mail service to East Asia and Australia: the *Prinz-Regent Luitpold* and the *Prinz Heinrich*. Both had been built by Schichau in Danzig and reached a cruising speed of 13.5 knots. The picture just below shows the *Prinz Heinrich* after being rebuilt in 1909, in which the superstructures were raised and the displacement increased to 6636 tons. The ship, which measured 144 meters overall, now carried 163 first-class, 62 second-class and 48 steerage passengers.

Bottom: The 10,881-ton, 166-meter *Prinzess Irene*, built by Vulcan of Stettin in 1900. was the last Lloyd steamer of the *Barbarossa* Class (see next two pages). She had accommodations for 2354 passengers, 1954 of them in steerage. Lying in New York in 1914, she was commandeered by the U.S. Navy in 1917. Lloyd bought the ship back in 1922 and used her on the New York line as of 1923 under the name of *Bremen*. Renamed *Karlsruhe* in 1928, she was scrapped at Bremerhaven in 1932.

Above: The *Barbarossa,* delivered to Lloyd by Blohm & Voss in 1897, was the type ship, though not the first ship, of the *Barbarossa* class (see next page). With an overall length of 166 meters, she displaced 10,769 tons, and her two quadruple-expansion engines, producing 7000 PS in all, moved her at 14.5 knots. Interned in New York in 1914, she served under the U.S. flag as of 1917.

Right: The *Bremen* of the *Barbarossa* Class, built by F. Schichau in Danzig, came into service in 1897. In the catastrophic fire at the Lloyd pier in Hoboken, which cost some 300 lives, she was burned out along with two other Lloyd steamers. This picture shows here after being repaired and rebuilt. She was turned over to Great Britain in 1919.

The seven ships of the *Barbarossa* Class — *Friedrich der Grosse, Barbarossa, Königin Luise, Bremen, König Albert, Grosser Kurfürst* and *Prinzess Irene* — were put into Imperial mail service to East Asia and Australia by the Norddeutsche Lloyd. In the summer months, though, when there was little traffic in that area but much on the North Atlantic, they ran to America.

All seven steamers were twin-screw ships built in German shipyards. The first four made about 15 knots, the last three 16. The *Barbarossa* ships could carry the enormous number of almost 2000 steerage passengers, also had a large freight capacity, and carried some 150 to 250 first- and second-class passengers.

The *Friedrich der Grosse* was, in 1896, the first German ship displacing over 10,000 tons. Only six British and American transatlantic high-speed liners were bigger, and in the East Asian and Australian trade the *Barbarossa* steamers were far and away the largest of all ships used there by any international firm for many years.

The Hapag, also briefly involved in the subsidized mail lines, put four ships of the *Barbarossa* Class into service too. They were the *Hamburg* and the *Kiautschou* and the larger *Blücher* and *Moltke* (see pages 67 and 92-93).

The picture below shows the Lloyd steamer *Grosser Kurfürst*, built by Schichau in Danzig in 1900, off Bremerhaven. At 13,812 tons and 177 meters in overall length, she was clearly bigger than the other *Barbarossa* ships, and had a capacity of 144 first-class, 281 second-class and 2373 steerage passengers.

The *Corrientes*, shown above and built by Mitchell in Walker-on-Tyne, near Newcastle, and the *Amazonas* at right, delivered by Blohm & Voss in 1890, were typical freight and passenger steamers used by Hamburg-Süd for service to the east coast of South America. The 1938-ton *Corrientes* had a registered length of 87 meters, made ten knots with an 800-HP compound engine, and carried 30 first-class and 260 steerage passengers. The *Amazonas* displaced 3075 tons and was 100 meters long. She made 12 knots and had a capacity of 40 first-class, 14 second-class and 214 steerage passengers.

The *Antonina* of 1898 (4010 tons, 304 passengers, 276 of them in steerage) shown at upper left after being bought by the Hapag in 1904, the *Tijuca* of 1899 (4801 tons, 450 passengers, 400 of them in steerage), at lower left, and the *Tucuman* of 1895 (4661 tons, 464 passengers, 400 of them in steerage), all built by Blohm & Voss, were Hamburg-Süd steamers on the South American run. The *Palatia*, built at Stettin in 1895 (6687 tons, 2573 passengers, 2349 of them in steerage), shown at Bremerhaven on 1900 carrying troops bound for China, was one of the Hapag's five smaller P-steamers (see page 54).

Around 1900 the passenger steamers were quite the equal of the most impressive new luxury hotels on land. The best architects and artists of the time were responsible for their furnishings. The style of the transatlantic steamers was aimed above all at American tastes. Although almost all the ships on the North Atlantic route before World War I were owned by European firms, Americans were always the great majority of the first-class passengers. and they were not devoted to using the ships of any one particular nationality, whereas the British, French, Italians, Germans, etc., preferred the steamships of their own country. Thus all the shipping firms took the Americans' wishes into consideration, and there were no great national differences in the style of interior decor. At most, the Italians and French who enjoyed a certain reputation for fashion and design in America might be allowed a little more extravagance. Generally, though, experiments with new styles and eccentric fads was avoided, and any changes in the basic style came in slowly. Steamship architecture was international.

To the extent that the superstructures went higher and higher from class to class, at least the first-class passengers moved farther and farther from the sea, finally floating high above it and being less and less aware of it. Heavy seas could no longer wash over the decks either

forward or aft. The provision of more and more space meant that one could forget the sea completely aboard a passenger ship.

At the beginning of the 20th Century, pompous historicity gradually passed out of style for the decor of passenger ships, and a style came in that was no longer dominated by rococo ornaments and plush

upholstery, though from today's standpoint it certainly does not seem at all simple or avant-garde. Even Georg Poppe, house architect of the Norddeutsche Lloyd, who had already decorated the River Class steamers most ornately, created a restrained style for the decor of the four-funnel high-speed steamers.

The contemporary color photos on

these two pages show first-class rooms on the promenade deck of the high-speed Lloyd steamer *Kronprinz Wilhelm,* (see pp. 60-65) built in 1901, which Poppe had designed; at lower left the sitting room with the access to the big light shaft of the dining room, which was several decks farther down, and above the smoking room with its broadly arched overhead windows.

Working with the leading passenger-ship builders of the time, Harland & Wolff of Belfast, Albert Ballin developed the concept of the huge but simple steamers of the second P Class that were used in the North Atlantic traffic. They proved to be extremely profitable. At about 13 knots they were very slow, and they carried only 162 first-class and barely 200 second-class passengers, but their steerages held almost 2400 emigrants. Thus the 12,891-ton *Pennsylvania*, when she was finished by Harland & Wolff early in 1897, was not the largest passenger ship afloat, but by the number of steerage passengers she was probably the largest emigrant ship, and her freight capacity of 14,500 tons also made her the biggest freighter in the world.

The 12,800-ton, 179-meter *Pretoria*, shown at right lying at anchor in the Elbe, was delivered to the Hapag by Blohm & Voss in 1898, the *Graf Wandersee*, shown above on the open sea, in 1899. The fourth and last two-screw steamer, the 13,023-ton *Patricia*, was also built in 1899 at a German yard, Vulcan of Stettin.

The painting by Antonio Jacobsen shown above shows the eleventh River Class ship of the Norddeutsche Lloyd, the *Havel*, built by Vulcan of Stettin in 1891, which ended the largest series of high-speed steamers ever contracted for by one shipping firm (see page 34). Like her sister ship, the *Spree*, she displaced 6963 tons and measured 141 meters, had a cruising speed of 18.5 and a top speed of almost 20, making her both bigger and faster than the other River Class steamers. But since the 12,500-HP engines and the necessary coal bunkers took up much more room, the steerage capacity was reduced to 384 persons, while the number of cabin passengers was raised slightly to 422. The *Havel*, already somewhat outmoded when put into service, was sold to Spain as early as 1898.

In one respect, though, the *Havel* provided pioneer service: She was the first ship with a post office on board. Postal employees could thus sort the mail aboard without losing time. On March 31, 1891 the *Havel*, first German-American sea post office and all, left Bremerhaven for the first time, carrying 83 sacks of mail.

The photo at lower right shows the 3169-ton, 98-meter two-screw steamer *Coblenz*, delivered to the Norddeutsche Lloyd by Blohm & Voss in 1897 and shown here tied up at a primitive-looking pier at Friedrich-Wilhelms-Haven on the north coast of New Guinea in 1911. At that time the *Coblenz* was running in the Imperial postal service on the South Sea line from Australia to Japan, and stopping at the German protectorate of the Bismarck Archipelago and Kaiser-Wilhelm-Land.

On the pier, in a white uniform, stands the ship's second officer, Carl Friedrich Christiansen of Föhr Island. The *Coblenz*, as was customary at the time, had an open bridge — there was shelter only in the charthouse. The awning used in the South Seas was placed some distance above, as can be seen here, so that the cooling breeze could blow over the charthouse. The row of windows before the bridge are from the sidewall of an Australian streetcar, which the crew had "obtained" at a depot in Sydney.

Right: The *Lyeemoon*, built for the Nissen firm of Hamburg in 1890 for the Chinese coastal trade, was one of the German passenger ships that never entered German harbors, seeing service in the East Asian trade instead. The 1925-ton *Lyeemoon* carried 184 passengers in three classes and provided line service from Canton and Hong Kong to Shanghai. In 1901 she was sold to the Hapag, which continued to use her on the same route.

The picture below shows Kaiser Wilhelm II, wearing an admiral's uniform, standing at the upper end of the gangway of the Lauenburg Elbe paddle steamer that bore his name. The *Kaiser Wilhelm II,* built by Klawitter of Danzig in 1892, was 45 meters long and could carry 392 passengers. Renamed *Hamburg* in 1919, she was run between Hamburg and Lauenburg by the Burmester Brothers, and was sold for towing service on the Weser in 1939.

The picture at upper right, taken shortly before World War I, shows Berlin Spree steamers tied up by the Jannowitz Bridge; from left to right, the *Fürst O. Bismarck* of 1904, the *Kronprinzessin Cecilie* of 1909, the *Odin* of 1906, and the ship launched in 1882 as the *Borussia* and rebuilt and renamed *Wotan* in 1912.

Left: The 86-meter express steamer *Borussia*, built in Holland in 1899, ran between Mainz and Cologne, carrying up to 1900 passengers, for the Köln-Düsseldorfer Linie. For the upstream voyage, covering some 17 kilometers per hour, she took twelve hours; for the downstream trip, at 28 kph, barely eight.

Left: The Lindau-based, 54-meter paddle steamer *Prinz-Regent* was put into service by the Royal Bavarian State Railroads in 1890. With a speed of 26.1 kph, she was the fastest ship on the Bodensee up to that time.

No other city on earth was so typified by passenger shipping and by one single line than Bremerhaven. Here hurrying businessmen or well-to-do vacationers became cabin passengers on high-speed liners for trips to America. Here many thousands of emigrants arrived on special trains every year, to travel on to a new homeland on large and small ships of the Norddeutsche Lloyd, the world's largest North Atlantic shipping firm. Here the Lloyd's land operations were centered too, here the steamers were repaired, loaded, provisioned and fueled. In almost every Bremerhaven family there was someone who sailed or worked for the Lloyd or was associated with it in some way. The city was almost identical to the Lloyd, at least until World War I.

Right: Three of the Norddeutsche Lloyd's four big four-funnel high-speed steamers are gathered in the Imperial Harbor at Bremerhaven; only the *Kaiser Wilhelm II* is missing. The *Kronprinz Wilhelm* has tied up in the foreground, the *Kronprinzessin Cecilie* and the *Kaiser Wilhelm der Grosse* follow, and the *Prinz Friedrich Wilhelm* (see page 94) can be seen far to the rear.

The four-funnel ships, put into service between 1897 and 1907 and also including the Hapag's *Deutsch-land*, marked the end of a long development. First of all, German ships were the biggest, fastest and most luxurious of their time. Thus German passenger shipping had reached the world's highest level, until then dominated by the leading British lines, and the German shipbuilding industry was now equal to the British as well.

Below: The unfortunate *Kaiser Friedrich* was ordered by the Norddeutsche Lloyd from the Schichau shipyards of Danzig, which were renowned for building fast torpedo boats, and was to enter high-speed service to New York along with the *Kaiser Wilhelm der Grosse*. The 12,841-ton, 183-meter *Kaiser Friedrich* went into service in 1898, but to the dismay of her builders and owners, stayed more than two knots below her contractually stipulated speed of 22 knots. For a year the builders tried everything in vain, including extending her funnels by four and a half meters for optimal boiler draft, to improve her speed. Finally the Lloyd refused to accept the ship. Until the *Deutschland* was put into service, the *Kaiser Friedrich* was chartered by the Hapag; then she lay unused in Hamburg harbor until 1912, when she was sold to a French firm.

Right: The Lloyd high-speed steamer *Kaiser Wilhelm II* (19,361 tons, 215 meters overall, 1535 passengers, including 468 in first class and 799 in dormitories), was delivered by Vulcan of Stettin in 1903. At the beginning of World War I she was interned in New York, confiscated by the U.S. Navy in 1917, laid up later and broken up at Boston in 1940.

Below: The Hapag's only four-funnel steamer was the *Deutschland*, also built by Vulcan; launched in 1900, she displaced 16,502 tons, was 209 meters long and carried 939 passengers. The picture shows her as the cruise ship *Victoria Luise*, as she was renamed after being rebuilt in 1911. After further rebuilding, including the removal of both forward funnels, she served as the emigrant ship *Hansa* until being scrapped in 1925.

The Norddeutsche Lloyd's *Kaiser Wilhelm der Grosse*, shown above in New York, was built by Vulcan of Stettin and, in 1897, opened a decade in which only German ships held the Blue Riband, the then-imaginary trophy for the fastest east-west crossing of the North Atlantic. (An actual Blue Riband Trophy was made in England in the 1930s).

The 14,349-ton, 198-meter *Kaiser Wilhelm der Grosse* was the first four-funnel steamer, and the world's largest ship when she was put into service in September of 1897. In the spring of 1898 the *Kaiser Wilhelm der Grosse* covered the stretch from the Needles off Southampton to Sandy Hook near New York in five days and twenty hours, averaging 22.29 knots. With this record run, she took the Blue Riband away from the Cunard liner *Lucania* and was now the world's fastest passenger ship.

The Hapag was determined to outdo the Lloyd and contracted with the Vulcan yards of Stettin for a larger high-speed steamer of the same type. On her maiden voyage via Cherbourg and Plymouth to New York in July of 1900, the *Deutschland* maintained an average speed of 22.42 knots, and the Bule Riband passed to Hamburg. Unlike the Lloyd steamers, the *Deutschland* had to deal with vibrations and engine trouble, and so she remained the Hapag's only high-speed steamer, as the line no longer cared to compete for speed records and, in fact, followed a different concept from then on (see page 88).

After the great success of the *Kaiser Wilhelm der Grosse* with the traveling public, the Lloyd placed the slightly larger *Kronprinz Wilhelm* in service in 1901. Averaging 23.09 knots, she won the Blue Riband in September of 1902, though the *Deutschland* won it

back again a year later. The *Kaiser Wilhelm II*, some 5000 tons bigger and even more luxuriously appointed than her two forerunners, went into Lloyd service in 1903. With an average 23.12 knots on the Cherbourg-Sandy Hook route in 1904, she beat the record of the *Kronprinz Wilhelm*, but not that of the *Deutschland*, which had meanwhile been raised to 23.15 knots. Only on the return trip, which did not count for the Blue Riband, since it is easier to cover thanks to the prevailing westerly winds, was the *Kaiser Wilhelm II* faster at 23.58 knots in 1906. Shortly after her sister ship *Kronprinzessin Cecilie*, with 45,000 HP the most powerful piston-engined steamer ever built, was put into service, the 24-knot British turbine-powered *Lusitania* brought the decade of German speed records to an end in the autumn of 1907.

Upper left: Departing for New York, the Lloyd high-speed steamer *Kronprinz Wilhelm* passes the Needles on its way out of Southampton. In the hilltop hut on the Isle of Wight is the radio station from which Guglielmo Marconi, the inventor of wireless telegraphy, first contacted a ship at sea in 1897. The 14,908-ton, 202-meter *Kronprinz Wilhelm* was built by Vulcan of Stettin in 1091 and had accommodations for 301 first-class, 300 second-class and 717 emigrant passengers (see page 53). On August 3, 1914 she left New York and was supplied with two 8.8 cm guns by the light cruiser Karlsruhe. As an auxiliary cruiser, she sank 15 merchant ships in the Atlantic until she ran low on fuel in April of 1915 and had to put into Newport News, where she was interned. After the united States entered the war in 1917, she was confiscated by the U.S. Navy, and scrapped in 1923.

Lower left: The Norddeutsche Lloyd's *Kronprinzessin Cecilie*, built by Vulcan of Stettin in 1907, was the last German four-funnel steamer. She displaced 19,360 tons and measured 215 meters, and her first-class capacity of 508 was the greatest of any Lloyd high-speed steamer. In 1914 she was interned in the USA, then commandeered in 1917 and used as a transport; after the war she was laid up, then scrapped at Boston in 1940.

Above: Emigrants enjoy the fresh air in their deck area near the bow of the *Kronprinzessin Cecilie*.

Below: Emigrants on the deck of the *Kronprinzessin Cecilie.*

Upper right: The 12,334-ton *Blücher*, seen here anchored in Norway's Geiranger Fjord while her passengers are on a land excursion during a Scandinavian cruise, and her sister ship *Moltke* were larger versions of the Norddeutsche Lloyd's *Barbarossa* Class (see page 48). Both ships were delivered to the Hamburg-America Line by Blohm & Voss in 1902, were 168 meters long overall and were moved by two screws at 15.5 knots. Aside from occasional cruises, the *Blücher* carried up to 333 first-class 244 second-class and 1614 steerage passengers on the Hamburg-New York route. In 1912, after being rebuilt and having luxurious new suites added on her boat deck, she entered the South American service. She was interned at Pernambuco when World War I began, commandeered by the Brazilian government in 1917, sold to France after the war and scrapped at Genoa in 1929.

Left: The *Moltke,* sister ship of the *Blücher,* also saw North Atlantic service for the Hapag, transferred to the Genoa-New York run in 1906, was interned in Genoa when World War I broke out, confiscated by Italy in 1915 and scrapped there in 1925.

The 3781-ton, 112-meter, 12.5-knot *Therapia*, delivered to the German Levante Line by Blohm & Voss in 1902, was that line's only newly-built passenger ship. In her luxurious cabins, 82 excursion passengers were taken to interesting ports in the eastern Mediterranean and Black Sea, to which the ship also applied freight service. In 1906 the *Therapia* was sold to the Norddeutsche Lloyd, which ran her from Marseille to the same ports.

The combined freight and passenger steamer *Elkab* (6118 tons, 131 meters, 10 knots, 110 passengers), built by Blohm & Voss in 1904, was one of five sister ships used by the Kosmos-Linie of Hamburg on their route to the west coast of America.

The *Prinzregent* (6341 tons, some 130 meters long, 13 knots) carried up to 111 first-class, 88 second- and 76 third-class passengers for the Deutsche Ost-Afrika-Linie in regular service from Hamburg around Africa.

The *Entrerios* (4395 tons, 120 meters, 10 knots), built at Sunderland by Laing & Sons in 1902, was one of the Hamburg-Süd's Santa Class freighters that could carry a large number of steerage passengers. Up to 800 emigrants and agricultural workers from Spain and Portugal, who returned home after the harvest season, were carried to the La Plata ports by the *Entrerios*.

Above: Like the *Elkab*,, the *Nitokris* (6150 tons, 131 meters, 11 knots), built by Blohm & Voss for the Kosmos-Linie in 1906, ran from Hamburg through the Straits of Magellan to Chile, Peru, Central America and the west coast of the USA. Her cabins carried 119 passengers in three classes, mainly along the American west coast.

Left: The *Schleswig* (6955 tons, 142 meters, 13.5 knots), built by vulcan of Stettin, could carry 1244 passengers, 950 of them in steerage and 230 in the first class, and was put into South American service by the Norddeutsche Lloyd in 1902, but transferred to Mediterranean service in 1904.

Right: The tender *Gruessgott* (725 tons, 63 meters, 1200 passengers), delivered to the Lloyd by Nüscke of Stettin in 1915, saw resort service from Bremerhaven to Helgoland from 1919 to 1929.

Below: The first turbine-driven German merchant ship was the famous 20-knot resort steamer *Kaiser*. Ordered from Vulcan of Stettin by Albert Ballin's Nordsee-Linie, the 1916-ton, 96-meter ship flew the Hapag flag from 1905 to 1934, except for minelaying service in the war, and with only one funnel and a speed of 16 knots as of 1922, carrying up to 2000 passengers between Hamburg, Helgoland and Sylt, before going into East Prussian service. In World War II she served as a minelayer again, was later sold to Poland and was scrapped at Stettin in 1954.

Above: The salon steamer *Föhr-Amrum* (211 tons, 37 meters, 10 knots), built by Howaldt of Kiel in 1908, put in fifty years' line service (until 1958) to Dagebüll, Wyk on Föhr and Wittdün on Amrum for the Wyker Dampfschiffs-Reederei.

Left: The *Bubendey* (849 tons, 68 meters overall, 12.5 knots, 756 passengers), built for the Hapag by the Oderwerke of Stettin in 1913, first served as the Southampton tender for the *Imperator* ships, entered the Helgoland service in 1919, was stationed at Southampton in 1930 as the Lloyd tender *Glückauf*, returned to service in 1948, was rebuilt as a one-funnel motor ship in 1954, served the Hapag as of 1960 as the *Kehrwieder*, ran regularly to Helgoland for the Schiffahrtsgesellschaft "Jade" as of 1961, was sold to Italy in 1963 and scrapped at Naples in 1986.

Lower left: The 400-ton, 58-meter paddle steamer *Delphin*, delivered to the Norddeutsche Lloyd by the AG "Weser" in 1905, carried 500 passengers between Bremerhaven and Wangerooge and sometimes to Helgoland, and was scrapped in 1950 after grounding off Wangerooge.

Upper left: The *Albatros* (214 tons, 37 meters, 10 knots, 405 passengers), built by Jos. L. Meyer of Papenburg in 1912 for the Vereinigte Flensburg-Ekensunder und Sonderburger Dampfschiffs-Gesellschaft of Flensburg, was one of the typical fjord steamers. The picture shows her after World War II, bearing the funnel emblem of the Förde-Reederei. Taken out of service in 1969, the *Albatros* was towed to the Damp 2000 holiday center, there she was placed on land ad a tourist attraction.

Center: On October 1, 1903 the Danish State railways and the Friedrich Franz Railway of Mecklenburg opened the first international railroad ferry service on the Baltic Sea, running from Warnemünde to Gedser and making possible a direct rail link between Berlin and Copenhagen. The first German train ferry on this route was the *Friedrich Franz IV* shown here, a 1402-ton, 85-meter paddle steamer built by Schichau at Elbing in 1902 and running between Warnemünde and Gedser until 1926.

Lower left: Off Hook Terrace in Stettin lie the twin-screw steamers *Hertha* and *Odin* of the J.F. Braeunlich firm of Stettin. Both were built by the Stettin Oderwerke, the 1177-ton, 78-meter *Odin* in 1902 and the 1257-ton, 82-meter *Hertha* in 1905. They first provided line service from Stettin via Sassnitz to Trelleborg, and after train ferry service had been established between Rügen and Sweden in 1909, they ran only from Stettin to the resorts on the east coast of Rügen. The *Hertha* remained in Rügen service until World War II, while the *Odin* was also used in East Prussian service.

Lower right: The Hapag's cruise ship *Meteor*, built by Blohm & Voss in 1914, is seen anchored in the harbor of Valetta, Malta, during an Oriental cruise in 1911. The 3613-ton twin-screw steamer, 100 meters long at the waterline, ran at 12 knots and could carry 283 first-class cruise passengers. She was turned over to Great Britain in 1919.

Right: The *Prinzessin Victoria Luise* (4419 tons, 124 meters, 192 first-class passengers), built for the Hapag by Blohm & Voss in 1900, was the world's first ship built exclusively for cruises, but ran aground outside the harbor entrance at Kingston, Jamaica in 1906.

Center: In 1905 the Hapag bought the *Scot*, built at Dumbarton by Denny Bros., in England, renamed her *Oceana*, and placed her in high-speed winter service from Naples to Alexandria, Egypt, using her for cruises in the summer. After the loss of the *Princessin Victoria Luise*, the *Oceana* took her place as a full-time cruise ship. The *Oceana* (7859 tons, 169 meters overall, 392 first-class passengers) was sold to Canada in 1911.

The first cruises were run in the 1880s by British shipping firms, using older ships and going to Norway or the Mediterranean, and as of 1888 the Norddeutsche Lloyd sometimes sent a steamer on a pleasure cruise as well.

The first regular luxury cruises, though, were made by the Hapag; when their high-speed steamer *Augusta Victoria* (see page 37) could not lure enough passengers onto the inhospitable North Atlantic in the winter and would have to be laid up,

they tested the waters in 1891 by sending her on a 58-day "excursion" to the Mediterranean. This voyage, for which only first class was utilized, was such a success that the Hapag ran cruises with their fast steamers every year from then on, later going to Norway and other lands as well. Soon other ships, such as the *Blücher, Moltke* and *Hamburg,* were making cruises (see pages 67 and 91). In 1901 The Hapag placed the luxurious *Prinzessin Victoria Luise,* the first ship built only for cruises, in service;

the *Meteor,* offering lower prices, followed in 1904, likewise using only first class, and in 1911 the *Deutschland* was renamed *Victoria Luise* (see page 62) and became the world's largest pleasure ship.

The picture above shows the *Meteor* in the Norwegian fjords during a Scandinavian cruise in 1909. In the picture at right, she is passing through the Corinth Canal on an Oriental cruise.

After the Reichstag had decided in 1890 to subsidize a mail steamship line to German East Africa, the Deutsche Ost-Afrika-Linie was founded in Hamburg, directed by Adolph Woermann, who had much experience in West African shipping.

Their Imperial mail steamers ran through the Suez Canal and via Aden to Zanzibar and Dar Es Salaam, then on via Mozambique to Lourenço Marques and later to Durban. Freight carrying played the leading role. During the entire year of 1890, the DOAL carried only 1033 passengers between Europe and Africa, mostly colonial officials and businessmen. Only in 1896 were larger steamers capable of carrying over 100 passengers, the *Herzog* and *König*, put into service.

When the government subsidies were extended for fifteen years in 1900, the DOAL establish line service around Africa in both directions, also serving the most important South American ports. The freight and passenger steamer *Kronprinz*, built by Blohm & Voss in 1900 and shown above before the fish auction market in Altona, opened this new route in 1901. She displaced 5645 tons, measured 125 meters at the waterline, attained 13.5 knots with her twin screws, and could carry 72 first-class, 56 second and 60 third-class passengers. Laid up at Lourenço Marques in 1914, she was commandeered by Portugal in 1916.

Lower left: The *General,* built by Blohm & Voss in Hamburg in 1911, was the Deutsche Ost-Afrika-Linie's largest ship before World War I, and also provided line service from Hamburg around Africa. She displaced 8063 tons and measured 137 meters long, ran at 13.5 knots and carried 155 passengers in first, 40 in second and 88 in third class. Underway to the Suez Canal in the Mediterranean when the war broke out, she was ordered to Constantinople by the Imperial Navy, where she was stationed as hospital ship and tender to the battle cruiser *Goeben,* which had been turned over to Turkey. In 1918 the *Goeben* was turned over to France.

Above: The 6341-ton, 127-meter *Admiral,* built by Blohm & Voss in 1905, was a sister ship of the *Prinzregent* (see page 68) and, like her, saw service on the DOAL line around Africa. In 1916, laid up at Lourençço Marques, she was confiscated by Portugal.

Left: The *Tabora,* an 8022-ton sister ship of the *General* built by Blohm & Voss, was placed in service by the DOAL in 1912 and had a capacity of 116 passengers in first, 112 in second and 88 in third class. Laid up at Dar Es Salaam in 1914, she was sunk there by cruisers of the British blockading squadron in 1916.

Above: The 9060-ton *Derffliger*, one of the eleven East Asian steamers of the Field Marshal Class, was built for the Lloyd in 1908 and ran onto rocks in the Yellow Sea in 1929, but could be towed off after the passengers had been removed.

Below: The 6598-ton *Rugia*, built for the Hamburg-Amerika Line's East Asian service in 1905 and accommodating 933 passengers, ran aground on the coast of Uruguay in 1923 and could be floated off only several months later.

Right: The 4689-ton, 808-passenger *Prinz Sigismund*, built at Rostock in 1903 for the Hapag, was one of the seven Central American steamers on the Prince Class. In the background are a high-speed Hapag steamer and the five-masted ship *Preussen*.

Right: The *Fuerst Bismarck*, 8332 tons and 148 meters long overall, was built by Fairfields of Glasgow in 1905 and is shown here entering the Elbe from the sea in winter. She went into Hapag passenger and freight service from Hamburg to Cuba and Mexico in 1906, and could carry up to 229 passengers in first, 40 in second and 841 in third class. In 1914, renamed *Friedrichsruh*, she was laid up at Hamburg, and in 1919 she was turned over to Britain.

In 1903 two large screw steamers, the *Servian* and *Scotian*, were launched at the Harland & Wolff yards in Belfast for the Wilsons & Furness-Leyland Line. At that time, though, the firm had already withdrawn the contract, and so the two steamers were laid up unfinished. In 1906 the Hapag bought the ships for their North Atlantic service, and after they were finished they were placed in service in 1907, the *Servian* as *President Lincoln*, and the *Scotian* as *President Grant*. They had the characteristic profile of many Harland & Wolff ships, with the bridge set

apart from the other superstructure, and were the only large passenger ships in the world with six masts. They resembled the *Pennsylvania* and her sister ships in general (see page 54), and displacing 18,074 and 18,072 tons and measuring 188 meters overall, they were noticeably larger, and at 14.5 knots, somewhat faster. With a freight capacity of over 20,000 tons and room for 3800 passengers, 3350 of them in third class and steerage, the *President Lincoln* and *President Grant* were both the biggest freighters and the biggest emigrant ships in the world.

Both steamers lay in New York when World War I broke out in 1914 and, after the United States entered the war in 1917, were used as U.S. Navy troopships. The *President Lincoln* met her end in the Atlantic in 1918 after being torpedoed by a German U-boat; the *President Grant* survived the war, served later as a passenger ship and again as a transport in World War II, and was scrapped in 1951.

The pictures show the *President Grant* off Cuxhaven at lower left and the *President Lincoln* in the north Atlantic above.

Right: The twin-screw steamer *Cap Finisterre*, built by Blohm & Voss for Hamburg-Süd and measuring 180 meters overall, was placed in service in 1911. She displaced 14,503 tons and was the biggest and, at 16.5 knots, the fastest ship on the South Atlantic, as well as the most comfortable, thanks to her particularly luxurious interior decor designed by the Hamburg architect Emil R. Janda. The *Cap Finisterre* could carry 297 passengers in firstclass, 222 in second and 870 in third. She was laid up at Hamburg when World War I broke out and turned over to the USA in 1919.

Lower left: In the days of coal-fired boilers, filling the bunkers was always a dirty job, and a time-consuming one as well when the fuel had to be carried aboard in baskets by hundreds of workers. This picture shows the Hapag steamer *Cleveland* being coaled at Nagasaki.

Above: On April 25, 1907 the first *Cap Arcona* was launched at the Blohm & Voss yards in Hamburg for Hamburg-Süd; at 9832 tons it was that line's bit a year before, the *Cap Arcona* helped the Hamburg-Süd catch up with her British, French and Italian competitors in terms of the

size and speed of their ships providing service to South America. Both were twin-screw steamers with one funnel and reached 15 knots. The *Cap Arcona* carried 244 passengers in first class, 110 in second and 404 in third. She was laid up at Villagarcia in 1914 and turned over to France in 1919.

Upper left: Passengers on the foredeck of the Hapag cruise ship *Victoria Luise*, formerly *Deutschland* (see pages 62 and 74).

Lower left: For decades the long, narrow, open-sided promenade deck, covered by the boat deck above, was a typical feature of all large passenger ships. This picture shows first-class travelers on the promenade deck of the Lloyd steamer *Kronprinzessin Cecilie* (see pages 60-66).

Upper right: First-class passengers' children aboard the *Victoria Luise* during a cruise.

Lower right: Third-class passengers and their children on their afterdeck area of the Hapag luxury steamer *Vaterland* (see pages 98ff).

Left page, upper left: Count Waldersee, the commander of the international expeditionary forces sent to China, arrives at Shanghai aboard the Lloyd steamer *Sachsen* on September 21, 1900. Upper right: Enrico Caruso, the world-famous tenor (sitting in the middle), underway to appearances in the USA, on the deck of the *Kaiser Wilhelm II* in September of 1903. Lower left: Prinze Heinrich, coming home from his South American trip, aboard the *Cap Trafalgar* in 1914; seated, from left to right, Prince Heinrich, Frau Konsul Staudt, Princess Heinrich, standing, Adjutant Kapitänleutnant von Tyska, Dr. Braumüller, Fräulein Staudt, Imperial Ambassador to Argentina von dem Bussche-Haddenhausen and Commodore Langerhannss, sitting below, Karl von dem Bussche-Haddenhausen and the well-known writer Fedor von Zobeltitz. Lower right: The painter Heyduck (far left), the critic Alfred Kerr (with full beard), and the silent film star Asta Nielsen (second from right) on the promenade deck of the *Vaterland* in 1914.

Above: On the tender *Willkommen*, the suitcases and cabin trunks of the passengers were brought to the *Imperator* as she lay in the roadstead.

Left: The 24,851-ton, 215-meter twin-screw steamer *Kaiserin Auguste Victoria* was delivered to the Hapag by the Vulcan yards of Stettin in 1906, supplanting the *Amerika* as the world's largest ship. The *Kaiserin Auguste Victoria* could carry 3006 passengers, 666 of them in first class and 2046 in third class and steerage, and had a 593-man crew. She provided line service to New York until 1914, was laid up at Hamburg during the war, turned over to Britain in 1919, put into service as the *Empress of Scotland* in 1921 and scrapped in 1930.

After the bad experiences with the record-breaking *Deutschland* (see pages 62ff), which was shaken by unpleasant vibrations at top speed, losing her rudder and sternpost in mid-Atlantic as a result, as well as consuming ungodly amounts of coal, as did all high-speed steamers, Albert Ballin switched to a new concept that the British White Star Line had begun in 1901 with the *Celtic* Class. He had the *Amerika* built by Harland & Wolff of Belfast in 1905. At almost the same length as the *Deutschland*, she was built wider and higher and displaced a noteworthy 5700 tons more. Since she ran at an economical 17 to 18 knots, she consumed only half as much coal. For a transatlantic passage she took one or two days longer than the high-speed steamers. To bring customers to the ship anyway, Ballin had it furnished with hitherto unknown lavishness and splendor: the first-class cabins and state suites were luxurious and roomy, there were electric elevators and a winter garden with palms that radiated a bright tropical atmosphere, in contrast to the other rooms that featured a weightier elegance, and was furnished with basket chairs. First-class passengers had their own on-board Ritz-Carlton Restaurant at which, for the first time, they could order á la carte. Based on the renowned Ritz-Carlton restaurants in Paris, London and New York, the on-board restaurant had been planned and appointed by Swiss hotelier Cäsar Ritz and his architect Charles Mewès. Cooks and waiters were trained at the Paris Ritz, and the best chef in France served as the chief cook.

This concept of a moderately fast but grand and opulent luxury liner proved to be very successful, and was continued with the Hapag's *Kaiserin Auguste Victoria* in 1906 and the Lloyd's *George Washington* (see pages 94ff) in 1909.

The picture at lower left shows the Hapag's 213-meter, 22,225-ton *Amerika*, built by Harland & Wolff in 1905 and for several months the world's largest ship. She was also the last major German ship to be built outside Germany. She had room for up to 2975 passengers, 531 of them in first class and 2190 in third class and steerage. She was interned in Boston in 1914, confiscated by the USA in 1917, used as a transport and passenger ship under the American flag in the following years, laid up and rebuilt several times, and finally scrapped at Baltimore in 1958.

The contemporary postcards shown above depict the first-class staircase and children's room of the Hapag luxury liner *Amerika*.

89

In 1909 the Hapag put two more big twin-screw steamers in service on the North Atlantic route. The 16,960-ton *Cleveland*, 185 meters long overall, was built by Blohm & Voss, the slightly smaller *Cincinnati* by F. Schichau of Danzig. The cruising speed of both ships was 15.5 knots. They had accommodations for almost 300 passengers in first and 350 in second class. In the lower-priced accommodations a development that had begun around the turn of the century appeared. The prosperity of even the lower strata of society had improved, and so the shipping firms began to offer a new third class along with the steerage, where the emigrants and lower bourgeois were housed no longer in large salons, but in the modest comfort of multibed cabins. Thus the *Cleveland* and *Cincinnati* could carry almost 1900 steerage passengers but, like other Hapag steamers, already had a third class with a capacity of almost 500.

The *Cleveland* was laid up at Hamburg when the war began, turned over to the USA in 1919, bought back by the Hapag in 1926 and used as a passenger ship until she was scrapped in 1933. The *Cincinnati* lay in Boston in 1914, was confiscated by the USA and used as a troop transport in 1917, and was sunk by a German U-boat on the Atlantic in 1918.

The pictures show the *Cincinnati* at left and the *Cleveland* leaving Cuxhaven above.

The next two pages reproduce a painting by Michael Zeno Diemer, showing the Hapag steamer *Hamburg* off Rejkyavik during a northern cruise in 1905. The *Hamburg* and her sister ship *Kiautschou*m both put into service in 1900, belonged to the *Barbarossa* class (see page 48) and were intended, like the rest of that class, for the Imperial mail steamship lines to East Asia and Australia run in cooperation with the Lloyd. After the Hapag withdrew from this service in 1904, she sold the *Kiautschou* to the Lloyd, which renamed her *Princess Alice,* and used the *Hamburg* on the North Atlantic and for cruises. The 10,532-ton *Hamburg*, built by Vulcan of Stettin, measured 159 meters long overall, ran at 15 to 16 knots, and carried 199 passengers in first class, 86 in second and 80 in third, plus an additional 1700 in steerage on the North Atlantic route. Interned in New York in 1914, she was taken over by the U.S. Navy in 1917, was used as a passenger ship after the war, and was scrapped in the USA in 1928.

The picture above shows the *Berlin*, built by the AG "Weser" of Bremen in 1909, in Genoa harbor, from where she traveled to New York in the Norddeutsche Lloyd's Mediterranean service. At 17,324 tons, she was the largest ship on this route before World War I. She reached 17.5 knots, was 187 meters long overall, and could carry 3231 passengers, 304 in first class and 2719 in steerage. In 1914, serving as an auxiliary cruiser, she laid mines in the Irish Sea, put into Trondheim when her coal ran out, and was interned there; she was turned over to Britain in 1919 and sold for scrap in 1931.

Lower right: After the great success of the big Hapag luxury ships *Amerika* and *Kaiserin Auguste Victoria* (see pages 88ff), the Norddeutsche Lloyd decided to have a steamer of this type built for the North Atlantic service. The 25,570-ton *George Washington*, 220 meters long overall, is shown above. She was built by Vulcan of Stettin in 1909, had a cruising speed of 19 knots, and was the biggest Lloyd steamship before World War I. She had a 586-man crew and accommodations for 518 in first class, 465 in second, 452 in third and 1449 in steerage. The Lloyd had hired Bruno Paul of the modern-art

Vereinigte Werkstätten for the interior decor, and this understated, modern luxury decor won much approval from press and public alike.

When the war began. the *George Washington* was interned in New York; she was commandeered by the U.S. Navy in 1917, used later as a passenger ship, and again as a transport in World War II under the American flag, and scrapped at Baltimore in 1951.

Upper right: The 17,082-ton, 187-meter *Prinz Friedrich Wilhelm*, almost a sister ship of the *Berlin*, but intended for the Bremerhaven-New York route, was built for the Norddeutsche Lloyd by Joh. C. Tecklenborg of Geestemünde in 1908. She had accommodations for 2466 passengers, 364 of them in first class and 1726 in steerage, and cruised at 17 knots. She was laid up in Norway in 1914, turned over to Great Britain in 1919, and scrapped in Genoa in 1930.

Below: The 9630-ton, 155-meter *Prinz Ludwig*, built by Vulcan of Stettin in 1906, joined the somewhat smaller *Prinz Eitel Friedrich*, which had been put into service two years before, in the Norddeutsche Lloyd's Imperial mail service to East Asia. She made 15 knots and could carry 763 passengers, 148 in first class, 453 in third and steerage. She was turned over to Britain in 1919 and scrapped at Bremerhaven in 1925.

From the turn of the century to World War I, the Hapag and the British White Star and Cunard Lines carried on a steadily escalating competition, in the course of which they tried to outdo each other with more and more gigantic luxury liners. In 1900 the world's largest ship was the 17,000-ton White Star steamer *Oceanic,* but a year later the same line's *Celtic* was the first to exceed 20,000 tons; the Hapag followed with *Amerika* and *Kaiserin Auguste Victoria* (see pages 88ff), and in 1907 the Cunard high-speed steamers *Lusitania* and *Mauretania* broke not only speed records but, at over 30,000

tons, size records as well. The White Star Line replied in 1911 and 1912 with the slower but more than 45,000-ton four-funnel luxury liners *Olympic* and *Titanic.* The high point, and also the endpoint, of this hasty development was attained by the Hapag with the three gigantic 55,000-ton liners of the *Imperator* Class, which were to remain the world's largest ships for twenty years.

The reproduction of Hans Bohrdt's gouache of the *Imperator,* owned by the Museum of Hamburg History, was launched at the Hamburg branch of Vulcan of Stettin on May 23, 1912, after Kaiser Wilhelm II had christened

her personally. The apparently over-size eagle on a globe was actually attached to the bow of the ship in that form and size. During a bad Atlantic storm in the spring of 1914, though, this masterpiece of Wilhelmine design, some four times a man's height including crown and globe, lost its wings, and the rest of the bronze sculpture was removed.

The photo of the four-screw steamer *Imperator* at right, taken on September 25, 1911, eight months before her launching, clearly shows the building style of the time, with overlapping rows of plates held together by countless rivets.

96

The 52,117-ton 280-meter *Imperator* set off on her maiden voyage from Cuxhaven to New York on June 20, 1913. Her four turbines moved her at a cruising speed of 23 knots, with her high speed about one knot higher. Like the *Vaterland*, she was not about to set new speed records, but she ran faster than almost all other passenger liners and came close to the 26 knots of the Blue Riband holder, the *Mauretania*. The *Imperator* could carry more passengers than any ship before or since. She had accommodations for 4248 people in all, 908 in first class, 606 in second, 962 in third and 1772 in what was called fourth class, where the steerage passengers were no longer accommodated in dormitories but in simple multiple-bed rooms. A crew of 1180 served the machines and the people on board.

When the war began, the *Imperator* was laid up at Hamburg; she was turned over to the U.S. Navy in 1919 and the British a year later, put into service by Cunard as the *Berengaria* in 1921, and sold for scrap in 1939.

The *Vaterland*, delivered to the Hapag by Blohm & Voss on May 1, 1914, is shown below. At 54,282 tons and 290 meters overall, she was the

largest passenger liner ever to fly the German flag. Her crew numbered 1234 men, and she could carry 3897 passengers, 980 in first class, 535 in second, 850 in third and 1532 in fourth. The *Vaterland* was interned in New York in 1914 and confiscated by the U.S. Navy in 1917. From 1923 to 1932, and again briefly in 1934, the ran between New York and South-ampton as the United States Lines'

Leviathan, and in 1938 she was scrapped at Rosyth, Scotland.

The picture above shows the *Imperator* leaving Hamburg harbor, off the Altona steamship pier.

The picture on the next two pages shows the 56,551-ton, 291-meter *Bismarck* on the Elbe on March 30, 1922. Shortly afterward she was sent to Liverpool and turned over to the White Star Line, which ran her on the

Southampton-New York route as the *Majestic*. The *Bismarck*, last and largest ship of the *Imperator* Class, was launched at Blohm & Voss on June 20, 1914 and promised to the British government in 1919. Work on the ship had stopped during the war, after which she was finished by Blohm & Voss and sold to the White Star Line.

The furnishings of the *Imperator* Class liners exceeded anything before in roominess, grandeur and luxury. The first class took up most of the ship's length, stretching from the bridge to the last funnel; the second class extended aft from there. The third-class emigrants were housed at the stern, those of the fourth class or steerage forward in the hull. High above the bridge deck, instead of separate individual rooms, were a connected group of lavish halls that, especially on the *Vaterland*, were displaced to the ship's sides by the funnel shafts, offering splendid perspectives. From aft forward, they included the Ritz-Carlton Restaurant, from which an open platform and several steps led to the more than six-meter-high winter garden, then the main landing with its elevators and stairwells at the sides, from which one could enter the hall that was also used as a ballroom; it measured 23 meters long, 17 meters wide and 7 meters high and was illuminated by indirect artificial light from the domed ceiling. The ladies' salon was farthest forward. Farther down in the hull was the ship's largest room, the dining room, more than eight meters high and crowned by a built-in dome, plus the swimming pool in Pompeian style.

The picture on the page at left shows the ballroom of the *Imperator*, that above shows its large dining room, while that at lower left depicts the plainly furnished steerage dining room of the *Vaterland*. On the next two pages we see the electric elevators of the *Imperator* and their operators, the barbershop of the *Vaterland*, and the swimming pool down in the hull of the *Imperator*, 2.4 meters deep, with a surface area of 57 square meters, and extending through three decks.

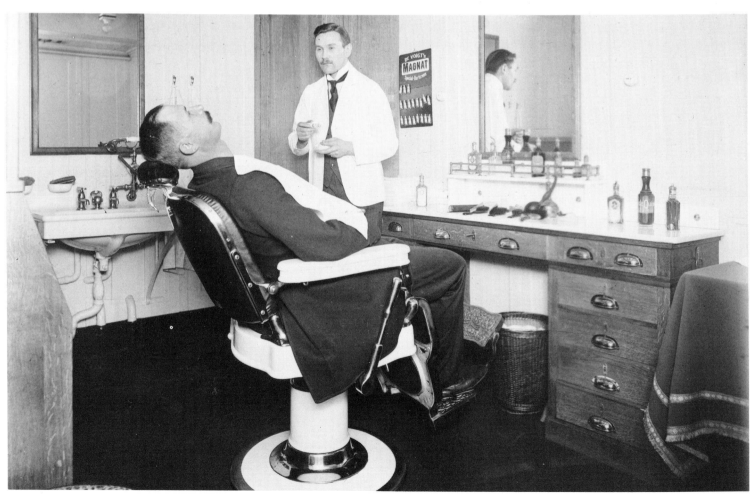

The picture at left shows third-class passengers at the stern of the *Imperator;* that above shows the *Vaterland* leaving the Steuben Pier at Cuxhaven for New York, with steerage passengers on deck.

The *Imperator*, with its arrogant eagle perched on a globe constituting a frighteningly clear symbol of German imperialism, and her sister ships exemplified, more vividly than any other technical product, the high point of a continuing, fateful development that had gone on in the industrial nations since the 1860s, typified by an ideology of uncritical belief in progress and unlimited economic expansion, ruthless exploitation of foreign lands and their own peoples, ever-increasing desire for ostentation and nationalistic arrogance, which led directly to World War I. In this egomaniacal striving for worldwide prestige, the Germans stood out particularly, under their brash Kaiser, who loved to put on his admiral's uniform and christen warships, and his Grand Admiral von

Tirpitz, who threatened Great Britain with a battle fleet armed to the teeth. The great German shipping firms also took part, with more and more bombastic ships, in the great game, giving their blessing to German imperialism by bestowing more and more Imperial and nationalistic names on their liners and ornamenting them with busts and portraits of His Imperial Majesty.

After the war broke out, though, the "greatest ships in the world" and the other steamships of the "greatest shipping company in the world", the Hapag, and the second greatest, the Lloyd, to say nothing of all other German merchant ships, were suddenly silent. They were held in German harbors by the British blockade, surprised in suddenly hostile foreign ports and confiscated by the

enemy, sent out to sea or, in great numbers, laid up in neutral ports, where most of them were commandeered when the country in question entered the war later. By the end of the war, German shipowners had lost 138 overseas passenger ships to sinking or confiscation. Ninety more followed when, according to the Treaty of Versailles, all German merchant ships over 1600 tons and half of the ships between 1000 and 1600 tons, including those under construction, were handed over to the victorious powers. The second greatest (after the British) merchant fleet in the world had ceased to exist.

The illustrations show, above, the *Vaterland* outward bound on the Elbe, and at right, the *Imperator* arriving in New York.

The first new German passenger ship built after the war was the *Bayern* (9014 tons, 148 meters overall, 12 knots), built by Vulkan of Bremen in 1921 and shown below. In the same year, the Hapag resumed passenger line service to New York with her. She carried 17 first-class and 762 third-class passengers, was used in the South American trade as of 1924, and was sold to France in 1936.

Bottom: The 7316-ton *España*, finished by the Howaldt works in Kiel at the beginning of 1922, was the Hamburg-Süd's first new passenger ship built after the war. Like her sister ships *La Coruña* and *Vigo*, also put into service in 1922, she had a

registered length of 126 meters and barely made 12 knots. She had room for 14 passengers in first class, 820 in third. In 1945 she was confiscated by the British in Norway, later put into service under the Russian flag, and broken up in Taiwan in 1974.

Above: The *General San Martin* (6079 tons, 120 meters, 12.5 knots), shown here in Norway's Näröfjord, was the first ship with which, in 1923, a German company ran cruises. She was built at the Reiherstieg shipyard in Hamburg in 1912 as *Professor Woermann* and captured off the Cape Verde Islands by a British cruiser in 1914. In 1921 the Hamburg-based shipping firm of the Ruhr industrialist Hugo Stinnes obtained the ship, which carried 121 passengers in first class and 88 in third, and placed

her in the South American trade as of 1922 as *General San Martin*. Used exclusively for cruises as of 1925, she was sold to Brazil in 1926, after the Stinnes lines were taken over by Deutsch-Austral and Kosmos.

The next two pages show the arrival of the *Cap Polonio* (20,576 tons, 202 meters overall, 18.5 knots) in Rio de Janeiro. With her three raked funnels and three-screw drive, she resembled the somewhat smaller *Cap Trafalgar*, which was 2000 tons smaller and which, after making several South American voyages before the war, was fitted out as an auxiliary cruiser and, in September of 1914, was sunk by the British auxiliary cruiser *Carmania*. With the *Cap Trafalgar*, the Hamburg-Süd introduced white funnels with red tops. The *Cap Polonio* was

launched by Blohm & Voss in the spring of 1914, shortly after the *Cap Trafalgar* was delivered, and after interruptions in construction, was put into service in 1915 as the auxiliary cruiser *Vineta*. A few days later she was taken out of service because her speed proved to be insufficient. In 1916 she was finished as the passenger ship *Cap Polonio* and immediately laid up, in 1919 she was turned over to Britain, and in 1921 the Hamburg-Süd bought her back. She left Habburg on her maiden voyage to Brazil and the La Plata ports in February of 1922, with accommodations for 356 passengers in first class, 220 in second and 949 in third. In 1931 she was laid up at Hamburg, and in 1935 she was sold to be scrapped in Bremerhaven.

All five of these turbine steamers were built for the combined German African service of the Deutsche Ost-Afrika-Linie and the Woermann-Linie, ownership of which had meanwhile passed more and more to Hapag and Lloyd. The *Ussukuma* (7765 tons, 132 meters overall, 11.5 knots, 264 passengers) of the DOAL was put into service in 1921; her sister ships *Adolph Woermann* (8577 tons, 291 passengers) and *Usambara* (8690 tons, 277 passengers), were 137 meters long overall, made 12 knots and were put into service in 1922 and 1923. In 1928 the African lines' first two-funnel ships, the *Ubena* (9554 tons) of the DOAL and the *Watussi* (9552 tons) of the Woermann-Linie, went into service. They were 141 meters long overall, made 13.5 knots, and carried 114 passengers in first class, 78 in second and 132 in third.

The two-screw steamer *Columbus* (32,354 tons, 236 meters overall, 18 knots, 1752 passengers in three classes), was built by Schichau of Danzig, made her maiden voyage from Bremerhaven to New York in April of 1924, and was Lloyd's flagship and Germany's largest ship for some years. On her the ocean flyers von Hünefeld, Köhl and Fitzmaurice, who were first to fly the Atlantic from east to west in April of 1928, returned to Germany and were greeted at Bremerhaven by a tremendous crowd, including aviators from all over Germany (above). In 1929 the *Columbus* was fitted with turbine engines; she now made 22 knots and, like the *Bremen* and *Europa,* was given shorter funnels.

Above: The *Stuttgart* (13,367 tons, 168 meters overall, 15 knots, 1105 passengers in three classes), finished by Vulcan of Stettin early in 1924, and her sister ship *München*, were the first new Lloyd ships built after the war for the North Atlantic service. As of 1937 the *Stuttgart* was only used for cruises; in 1938 she was sold to the Deutsche Arbeitsfront and used as a one-class ship for Kraft-durch-Freude vacation trips. In 1943, while used as a hospital ship at Gdingen, she was burned out.

Left: The *Sierra Ventana* (11,392 tons, 156 meters overall, 14 knots, 1093 passengers), delivered to the Lloyd by Vulkan of Bremen in 1923, took part in the South American service, as did her sister ships *Sierra Cordoba* and *Sierra Morena* (see page 161), and was sold to Italy in 1935.

The four twin-screw turbine steamers of the *Albert Ballin* Class built by Blohm & Voss were the most important Hapag ships in the North Atlantic service until World War II, and were made to suit changing demands by frequent rebuilding. At 16 knots, they were only moderately fast, but comfortably and pleasantly furnished ships that, thanks to the quiet running of their engines and the damping effect of their lateral

Frahm stabilizing tanks on the ships' movements in seaways, offered a pleasant voyage even in bad weather. The first two ships of this class, the *Albert Ballin* and the *Deutschland*, were finished in 1923 and were registered at 20,815 and 20,602 tons and 191 meters overall. They had accommodations for some 220 passengers in first class, 250 in second and 940 in third class. The 21,132-ton *Hamburg* and 21,455-ton *New York*, which differed from their forerunners in the number of their masts and the form of their sterns, were both 194 meters long and were placed in service

in 1925 and 1927. Because of American emigration restrictions and changes in traveling conditions, the passenger accommodations of all four ships were modified again and again. At first the third-class capacity was reduced to increase the second, then in 1928 a tourist class between second and third was added, to be expanded in 1930 at the expense of both second and third; in 1934 it completely replaced the second class.

The picture at the upper left shows the *Deutschland* on her test cruise on December 20, 1923. As on the *Albert Ballin*, her funnels were later raised,

and the open promenade under the bridge was enclosed by windows on all the ships.

The *Albert Ballin* is shown at lower left after being rebuilt in 1930, in which all four steamers received not only new low funnels but also new engines that produced 19-knot speeds. The black-white-red funnel top was introduced officially on all Hapag ships on January 1, 1927, after merger with the Deutsch-Austral and Kosmos lines.

Above: The *Hamburg* is docked at the Hamburg overseas pier on "Seafaring Day" in 1935.

From the autumn of 1933 to the spring of 1934, the Hapag withdrew one ship of the *Albert Ballin* Class at a time from the North Atlantic service for two months and equipped it with a new bow, some fifteen meters longer, at the Blohm & Voss floating dock. At this time the funnels were also lengthened again and new passenger accommodations were built. Their tonnage increased by 300 to 1000 tons, and despite the same engine performance right shows the *Hamburg* in her new state after lengthening.

In the picture at lower left, taken from aboard a fast torpedo boat, the *New York*, not yet rebuilt, is moving ahead at full speed on the high seas.

Above: Since Albert Ballin had been Jewish, the ship named after him was to be renamed *Hansa* in 1935, by order of the Nazis. This picture, taken in 1937, shows the *Hansa*, returning from America, at the Steuben Pier in Cuxhaven. The bulge in the side, behind which the bilge tanks were located, is easy to see.

All four ships of the *Albert Ballin* Class sank off the Baltic coast or in Baltic ports in 1945 after being bombed or hitting mines. Later all four wrecks were raised. While *Deutschland* and *New York* were scrapped, the *Hansa* was used as a passenger ship and the *Hamburg* as a whaling mother ship, both under the Russian flag. The latter was scrapped in 1977, the former in 1981.

The Ozean-Linie of Flensburg, a branch of the firm of H. Schuldt, began to carry passengers to Central America on her long-standing line of freighters in 1922. In 1924 the line put two new passenger ships into service on its Cuba-Mexico route, the *Rio Bravo* and *Rio Panuco*, which they had built at the Germaniawerft in Kiel. The *Rio Bravo* and *Rio Panuco* were modern twin-screw ships powered by diesel engines and capable of 12 knots. They were registered at 5946 and 5944 tons, with an overall length of 125 meters, and had accommodations for 88 first-class passengers. In 1926, accommodations for 84 second-class passengers were added. The interior decor was created by the Munich architect Paul Ludwig Troost. In joint service with the Hapag, the *Rio Bravo* and *Rio Panuco* ran from Hamburg to Havana, Vera Cruz and Tampico, Galveston and Houston. During the great depression the Ozean-Linie got into difficulties and sold both ships to the Norddeutsche Lloyd, which continued to use them on the Central American route as of 1931 without changing their names, but sold them to Hong Kong in 1934.

The five motor ships of the Monte Class built for Hamburg-Süd by Blohm & Voss differed from that firm's other ships in having neither a first nor a second class. Thus their third-class passengers could move freely on all decks, and for the first time, passengers in the lowest-priced category had not only large dining rooms but the use of roomy, though somewhat simply, furnished rooms such as a hall, a smoking room and a library. Half of the 2500 passengers were housed in cabins, the others in dormitories.

The Monte ships were registered at 13,625 to 13,913 tons, measured 160 meters overall, and were driven at 14 knots by two screws. The first ship of the class, the *Monte Sarmiento*, went into service in 1924, followed by the *Monte Olivia* in 1925, the *Monte Cervantes* in 1928, and the *Monte Pascoal* and *Monte Rosa* in 1931.

The picture above, taken on September 22, 1938, shows the *Monte Pascoal* arriving in Greenwich. Aboard are 800 former German soldiers who, led by the president of the Deutsche Soldatenbund, the duke of Saxe-Coburg-Gotha, were the guests of the British Legion in London for several days. In the war the *Monte Pascoal* was burned out at Wilhelmshaven, and in 1946, loaded with poison gas grenades, she was scuttled in the Skaggerak.

The 13,502-ton *Antonio Delfino*, shown at the upper left, and her sister ship *Cap Norte* were delivered to Hamburg-Süd by the Hamburg Vulcanwerft in 1922. These 160-meter, 13-knot twin-screw steamers carried up to 184 first-class and 334 third-class passengers from Hamburg to Brazil and the La Plata ports. From 1932 to 1934 they were chartered by the Norddeutsche Lloyd as *Sierra Nevada* and *Sierra Salvada*. Both were used as British troop transports during or after the war and were scrapped in Scotland in the mid-fifties.

Left center: The 13,750-ton *Monte Olivia* was the second ship of the Monte Class. When the war began, she broke through the British blockade on her way back from South America, became a naval barrack ship, was sunk in 1945 by a bomb attack on Kiel, and was scrapped.

Lower left: In 1923 the Hapag received two 11,343-ton one-screw steamers from the Howaldt Works in Kiel, the *Thuringia* and *Westphalia*, for the North Atlantic service. These 151-meter ships, which ran at 13.5 knots, were rebuilt in 1930, renamed *General San Martin* and *General Artigas*, and fitted with accom-

modations for 169 first-class and 392 third-class passengers on the South American route. The Hamburg-Süd chartered both steamers in 1934 and bought them in 1936. The picture shows the *General San Martin*, ex *Thuringia*, under the Hamburg-Süd flag.

Above: The Monte ships were built in expectation of a sharp increase in emigration to Brazil and Argentina, which did not materialize. Though the ships were kept busy in winter carrying Portuguese and Spanish farm workers to South America for harvesting, they had to find other uses during the summer. In 1925 the

Hamburg-Süd first offered low-priced cruises to Norway with the Monte ships, which offered only third class, and thus founded sea tours for the masses. The vacation trips on the one-class ships, which carried up to 1600 vacationers, were a great success, and every year the Hamburg-Süd increased the number of its tours, which also went to the Mediterranean as of 1928. The picture shows *Monte Sarmiento*, the world's largest motor ship when she was put into service, in the Näröfjord in western Norway. She sank in 1942 during an air attack on Kiel while in use as a naval barrack ship, and was scrapped a year later.

The *Monte Cervantes* was twice plagued by bad luck. During a northern tour she was holed in a thick icefield on the way from North Cape to Spitzbergen. She just managed to reach Spitzbergen and anchor there. The 1500 passengers were put ashore during the day while the Russian icebreaker *Krassin,* which had been called on for help, used its pumps to keep the *Monte Cervantes* afloat, and its crew spent several days plugging the leaks.

A year and a half later, the *Monte Cervantes* ran upon an uncharted rock while passing through the Beagle Channel off Tierra del Fuego, slid off it and began to sink. The 1117 passengers were put into the boats and later picked up by the Argentine steamer *Vincente Fidel Lopez* and taken safely to nearby Ushuaia, the southernmost town in the world. Meanwhile the *Monte Cervantes* was driven by heavy winds and strong currents into a group of rocks, where the captain grounded her stern. The bow floated free in the water but gradually sank deeper and deeper. On the next day, some of the luggage could be removed, and at high water, when the rocks around her were under water, the *Vincente Fidel Lopez* tried in vain to tow the *Monte Cervantes* off. The picture below shows this maneuver. On January 24, 1930 the *Monte Cervantes* suddenly began to move and capsized. The crewmen still on board jumped into the water and were picked up by a boat; only the captain could not save himself and drowned in the capsizing ship. The wreck, its stern still above water, was salvaged by an Italian firm in 1954 but then sank in the deep water of the Beagle Channel during the attempt to tow it to Ushuaia.

After the loss of the *Monte Cervantes,* the Hamburg-Süd ordered two new Monte ships from Blohm & Voss. They went into service in 1931 as the *Monte Pascoal* and *Monte Rosa.* The picture at right, taken from an airship on the same route, shows the *Monte Rosa* in the South Atlantic. She was turned over to Great Britain in 1945 and sank in the Mediterranean in 1954.

The two-screw steamer *Dresden*, shown at right, was built in 1915 by Vulkan of Bremen for the Norddeutsche Lloyd's Australian service as the *Zeppelin*. Laid up during the war, she was turned over to Britain in 1919. In 1927 the Lloyd bought back the 14,690-ton, 174-meter, 15.5-knot steamer, named her *Dresden*, and put her on the North Atlantic route, with accommodations for 280 passengers in the second cabin class, 288 in tourist and 280 in third. In 1934 she ran aground in Norway while on a KdF excursion and capsized. The wreck was broken up and scrapped.

The 15,286-ton, 174-meter *Berlin*, shown above, was built by Vulkan of Bremen in 1925. The Lloyd put the 16-knot twin-screw steamer into the North Atlantic service, where she carried 313 passengers in first class, 284 in second and 511 in third. The accommodations were changed in 1929 and again in 1932, and from 1934 on the *Berlin* also served as a cruise ship. She was a hospital ship in the war, hit a mine and sank off Swinemünde in 1945, and was later raised by the Russians rebuilt at the Warnow yards in Warnemünde, and used on the Black Sea as the passenger ship *Admiral Nachimov*. There she sank on August 31, 1986 after a collision

with a freighter, with a loss of 423 lives.

The picture above shows the 19,692-ton, 188-meter three-screw Hapag steamer *Resolute*, which could carry 353 passengers in first class, 232 in second and 264 in third and make 17 knots.

Next two pages: The Hapag steamer *Reliance* passes the Steuben Pier at Cuxhaven. This 19,527-ton, 187-meter steamer had accommodations for 374 passengers in first class, 222 in second and 252 in third. Like the *Resolute*, she had three screws and could make 17 knots.

The *Resolute* and *Reliance* had already been launched for the Hapag in 1914, before World War I began; the *Reliance* was built by Tecklenborg at Geestemünde as the *Johann Heinrich Burchard*, the *Resolute* by the AG "Weser" as the *William O'Swald*. Both were sold to Holland in 1916, with delivery dates after the war, and delivered to the Koninklijke Hollandsche Lloyd in Amsterdam in 1920, then resold in 1922 to the United American Lines of New York, which renamed them *Resolute* and *Reliance*. Because of American prohibition, they were put under the flag of Panama and run between Hamburg and New York in cooperation with the Hapag. In 1926 the Hapag bought both steamers and continued to run them on the same route without changing their names. From 1928 on they were used mainly, and from 1934 on only, for cruises; as of 1934 their hulls were painted white and they carried only 500 first-class passengers. The *Resolute* was sold to Italy in 1935, the *Reliance* was modernized and fitted with a thicker funnel in 1937. The *Reliance* burned at Hamburg in 1938, was laid up, then scrapped in 1941.

The picture at left shows vacationers on the deck of the *Resolute* during a Scandinavian tour in 1932; at right, costumed participants in a pirate festival are seen on the *Reliance* during a Caribbean cruise in 1926.

Upper left: The *Jan Molsen* (860 tons, 57 meters overall), built by the Stülckenwerft of Hamburg in 1925, was the first motor ship of the Hamburger Hafen Dampfschiffahrts-A.G. (Hadag). Driven by two screws, she made 11 knots. Her 2200-person capacity was used in harbor service as well as to Cuxhaven. Rebuilt several times, she was finally registered at 1217 tons. In 1967 she was sold to Italy and ran between Naples and Capri.

Center: The double-screw steamer *Frisia I* (504 tons, 52 meters, 11 knots, 830 passengers), built for the A.G. Reederei Norden-Frisia by Jos. L. Meyer of Papenburg in 1928, ran from Norddeich to Norderney and Juist and from Emden to Borkum, sometimes also to Helgoland, and was scrapped in Holland in 1967.

Lower left: The twin-screw turbine steamer *Cobra* (2132 tons, 88 meters overall, 17 knots, 1919 passengers), built by Vulcan of Stettin in 1926, was the first new ship built after the war for Hapag resort service and ran regularly from Hamburg and Cuxhaven to Helgoland and Hörnum on Sylt. In the war the *Cobra* was used as a minelayer. She capsized at Schiedam during a bomb attack in 1942 and was scrapped later.

Upper right: The train ferry *Schwerin* (3133 tons, 107 meters long, 161 meters of track, 800 passengers, 15.5 knots), built for the German railway system by Schichau at Elbing, replaced the *Friedrich Franz IV* (see page 72) on the Warnemünde-Gedser route in 1926. She was already set up to carry cars. In 1944 she was sunk by aerial bombs in Rostock, later raised and towed to Warnemünde, then scrapped in 1951.

Lower right: The twin-screw motor ship *Preussen* (2282 tons, 85 meters, 16 knots, 1158 passengers at night), built for the government transport ministry by the Oderwerke of Stettin in 1926 and run by J.F. Braeunlich, was a sister ship of the *Hansestadt Danzig*. In East Prussian service, she ran from Stettin to Pillau and Königsberg, was lengthened nine meters in 1934, and sank off Oland in 1941 while serving as a minelayer.

Below: The *Oceana,* seen here in Hapag colors around 1930, was built by Vulkan of Bremen for the Norddeutsche Lloyd in 1913, named *Sierra Salvada,* and put into the South American service with three other *Sierra* ships. Laid up at Rio when the war began, she was commandeered by Brazil in 1917. The Berlin merchant Viktor Schuppe bought the ship in 1923, named her *Peer Gynt,* and used her for cruises as of 1924, with Stettin as its home port, but soon got into financial difficulties and sent her to Italy at the end of 1925. Finally the Hapag bought the twin-screw steamer and put her into service as the cruise ship *Oceana* in 1928. The *Oceana* (8791 tons, 140 meters overall, 13 knots) was chartered to the Deutsche Arbeitsfront as a KdF ship in 1935 and

sold to them in 1938, turned over to Britain in 1945 and Russia in 1946, and scrapped in 1958.

Left: the *General von Steuben*, seen here arriving in Venice, was built by Vulcan of Stettin in 1923 and was called *München* when she ran in the Norddeutsche Lloyd's North Atlantic service with her sister ship *Stuttgart* (see page 117). The 168-meter, 15-knot *München* was burned out at New York in February of 1930, rebuilt by the A.G. "Weser" and given new funnels, and put back into service as *General von Steuben* in 1931. She was now registered at 14,690 tons and made 16.3 knots. As of 1935, with accommodations for 484 first-class passengers, she was used only for cruises; her name was shortened to *Steuben* in 1938, and on February 10,

1945, while carrying wounded and refugees from Pillau to Kiel, she was sunk by a Russian U-boat; some 3000 lives were lost.

Above: The 16,732-ton, 175-meter *St. Louis*, seen here leaving Hamburg harbor with help from a tugboat, became known to the world on a voyage from mid-May to mid-June 1939. With 937 Jewish emigrants fleeing from Nazi Germany and leaving all their property behind, the *St. Louis* ran from Hamburg to Cuba. The authorities there declared the visas, which had cost every passenger $1000, to be void and refused to let them enter. After a week of unsuccessful negotiations, the *St. Louis* left Havana and marked time off the Florida coast while Captain Gustav Schröder, the Hapag and Jewish

organizations telegraphed frantically in hopes of finding a solution, but the USA was not willing to let the refugees land either. Finally the *St. Louis* and her despairing passengers headed back toward Europe. Meanwhile the Gestapo had informed the Hapag that the passengers were to be sent to concentration camps after their return to Germany. Just a few days before the *St. Louis* reached the English Channel, Jewish organizations and Hapag director Holthusen persuaded the governments of Belgium, Holland, France and Great Britain to take the emigrants, and on June 17, 1939 the refugees disembarked in Antwerp. Gustav Schröder, the captain of the *St. Louis*, had treated his passengers in exemplary fashion and handled all the dramatic crises on

the ship with the help of a Jewish committee on board, received a letter of thanks from his rescued passengers in New York two weeks later.

The *St. Louis* and her sister ship, the 16,699-ton, 176-meter *Milwaukee,* were the first large Hapag passenger ships to be Diesel-powered. Both were built by Blohm & Voss in 1929, made 16.5 knots and carried 373 passengers in first class, 330 in tourist and 429 in third. They provided line service between Hamburg and New York, but were also used more and more often for cruises. The Milwaukee's hull was painted white later; as of 1936 she was used exclusively as a cruise ship with 600 first-class passengers. She is shown above in 1936, seen from the Süllberg in Blankenese. In 1945 she was turned over to Great Britain, was burned out at Liverpool in 1946 and scrapped at Glasgow in 1947.

Shortly before the war began, the *St. Louis* left New York, arrived in Murmansk on September 11, 1939, and finally reached Hamburg on January 1, 1940. Used as a naval barrack ship, she was beached at Kiel after being bombed in 1944; as of 1946 she lay off Altona, half burned-out and used as a hotel ship, until she was scrapped at Bremerhaven in 1950.

The picture at right shows vacationers on the boat deck of the *Milwaukee* during a cruise in 1939.

138

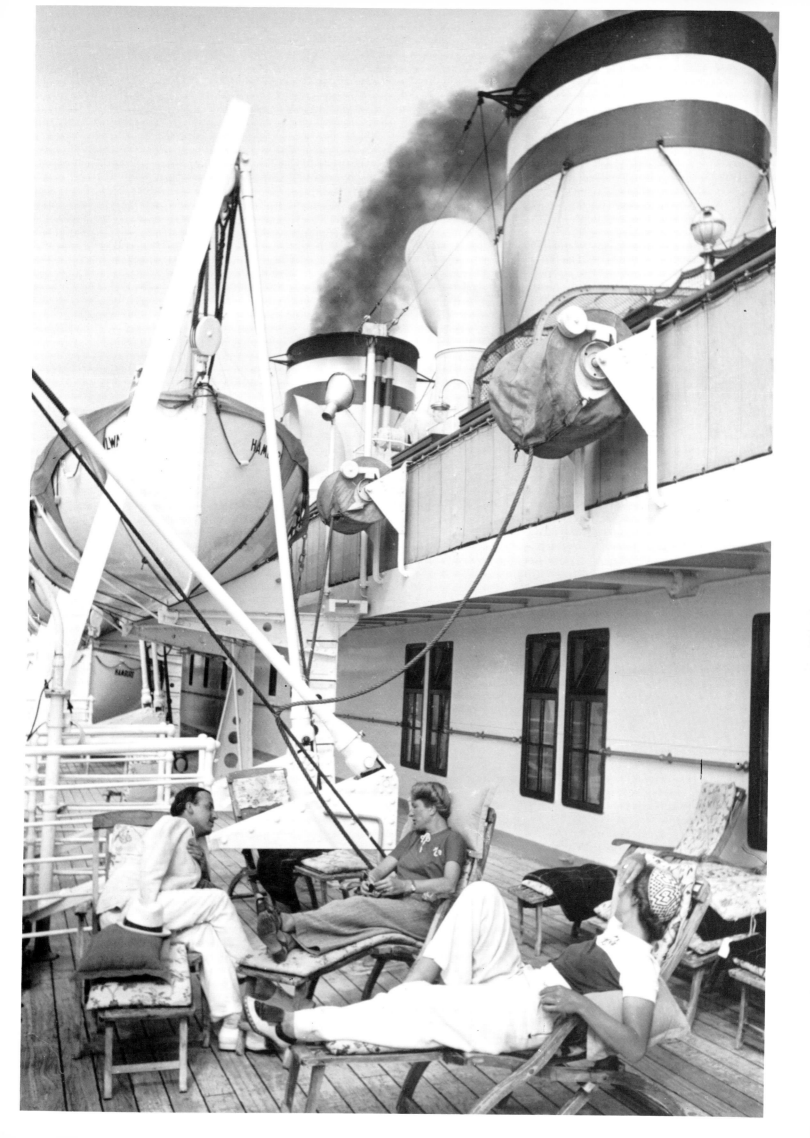

Like the *St. Louis* and *Milwaukee*, the *General Osorio*, shown above in the South Atlantic as seen from an airship, was a modern twin-screw Hapag motor ship. At 11,590 tons and 161 meters overall, she was somewhat smaller and did not run on the North Atlantic route, but rather to the La Plata ports. Built by Vulkan of Bremen in 1929 the *General Osorio* made 15 knots and had accommodations for 234 passengers in second class and 752 in third. In 1932, when line services of German firms were monopolized under the Nazis, she was chartered by the Hamburg-Süd, which bought her in 1936 and fitted higher funnels. In 1944, serving as a naval barrack ship, she was sunk at Kiel in an air raid, was raised but sunk again by bombs in 1945, raised again in 1947 and scrapped in Britain.

Two other Hapag motor ships were the *Orinoco* and *Magdalena*, both two-funnel passenger ships under 10,000 tons that were put into West Indian service in 1928. The latter grounded in 1935, was floated and rebuilt, including removal of the rear funnel, and renamed *Iberia*. The picture at right shows the bow of the *Milwaukee* during a 1938 cruise.

In November of 1927 the new Hamburg-Süd flagship, the 27,561-ton, 206-meter twin-screw turbine steamer *Cap Arcona,* set out on her maiden voyage to the La Plata ports. The *Cap Arcona,* built by Blohm & Voss, was the biggest, fastest and most luxurious steamer on the South Atlantic, and was exceeded in size and speed only in 1931 when the French Compagnie Sudatlantique's *L'Atlantique* was put into service in 1931. At twenty knots, she reached Rio de Janeiro from Hamburg in 12 days, Buenos Aires in 15. She carried 571 passengers in first class, 274 in second and 520 in the spartan third class, where there were only dormitories.

The luxurious first-class section of the *Cap Arcona* was popular among rich Argentinians and Brazilians, who often took their whole families to Paris for the summer. The big social rooms were located on the promenade deck. The 35-by-18-meter (630 square meters) dining hall, located behind the rear funnel, was five and a half meters high and extended through two decks. The walls were decorated in lemonwood and rosewood with green silk and three Gobelins. Twenty high windows opened onto the promenade deck. The picture below, taken from the music balcony one deck higher looking forward, shows first-class passengers having a party in the dining hall of the *Cap Arcona.* Forward of the dining hall, opening into each other and extending over 46

meters, were the ballroom and hall; farther forward was the 30-meter smoking room with a bar at the end.

One deck up, on the boat deck, was the winter garden shown above, decorated with a marble fountain surmounted by a bronze statue and furnished with the usual basket chairs; its domed glass ceiling rose above the sport deck between the middle and rear funnels.

The career of the *Cap Ancona* was glorious in peacetime, but its end in wartime was terrible. It spent most of the war as a naval barrack ship in

Gdingen, then known as Gotenhafen, then made three trips early in 1945 to carry 26,000 refugees westward, and anchored off Neustadt in Lübeck Bay with engine trouble on April 14. The Allies had already conquered most of Germany, and the only concentration camp still under Nazi control was that at Neuengamme near Hamburg. Following orders to let no living prisoners fall into Allied hands, the SS moved the inmates of Neuengamme to Lübeck on April 18. There columns of survivors from other camps in Mecklenburg and the

Magdeburg area arrived on foot at the same time. Many of the starving prisoners had died on the way, since they were given nothing to eat during the all-day marches, and whoever did not keep pace was shot.

On April 26, 1945 some ten thousand prisoners were loaded onto the *Cap Arcona*, the freighter *Thielbek* and the Hapag passenger liner *Deutschland* anchored in Lübeck Bay. The SS intended to let the people go down with the unseaworthy ships. Heinrich Bertram, the captain of the *Cap Arcona*, refused to

take the prisoners, as he had neither food nor water on board, but an SS command armed with machine pistols threatened to shoot him and left him no choice. Some 5000 prisoners were packed into the ship originally built for 1365 passengers. Indescribable conditions prevailed on board; there was scarcely anything to eat or drink, and no medicine for the many sick people. Hundreds died, and their naked bodies were stacked in a corner and thrown overboard every morning.

Meanwhile Hitler was dead; Führer-successor Dönitz had set up shop for the "government in business" at Flensburg, and at Neustadt no one knew whether the British troops already close to Lübeck or the approaching Red Army would occupy the city. Aboard the *Cap Arcona*, some 4600 prisoners were still alive, plus 500 guards and 70 crewmen, when British bombers flew one of their last missions against German ships on May 3, 1945. Around 2:30 P.M. they hit the anchored prison ships with explosive and incendiary bombs and guns. The *Thielbek* sank within twenty minutes with 2500 on board, the *Deutschland* followed shortly thereafter. The *Cap Arcona* burned furiously, then heeled over and capsized about an hour later. The hull, still about one-third above the shallow water, slowly burned out. Most of the prisoners suffocated or burned below decks, others swam desperately for their lives and sank into the icy water, exhausted and frozen. Only 350 men were saved from the *Cap Arcona*, and in all, more than eight thousand people lost their lives in this terrible inferno just four days before Germany's unconditional surrender. For years afterward, bodies and bones were washed up on the beaches of Lübeck Bay. The wreck of the *Cap Arcona*, lying off Neustadt, was scrapped on the spot in 1949-50.

Left: The 1300-square-meter sport deck above the dining hall of the *Cap Arcona*, on which evening parties were held in tropical waters, was divided into several sections including, among others, full-size tennis courts, shuffleboard and

horseshoe games, boxing and gymnastic facilities. In this picture, the airship *Graf Zeppelin* can be seen. From 1932 to 1937 it made regular three-day flights to Pernambuco (now called Recife) and Rio de Janeiro and often met the Hamburg-Süd liners, which followed the same route, at sea.

Above: One of the very few color pictures of the *Cap Arcona* shows her with the white hull stripe that was extended one deck farther down in 1934.

The pictures on the next two pages show, at upper left, the 35-meter, 430-passenger twin-screw steamer *Werner v. Siemens*, built by the Stettin Oderwerke in 1907, near the cathedral in central Berlin. She belonged to the Spree-Havel "Stern" Line and was fitted with a closed salon and a shorter funnel in 1925. At lower left is the 54-meter, 500-passenger train and car ferry *Schussen*, built in 1929, that ran between Friedrichshaven and Romanshorn on the Bodensee; at upper right is the 69-meter doubledeck salon steamer *Frauenlob* of the Köln-

Düsseldörfer Rheindampfschiffahrt before the German Corner at Koblenz; this ship, built as early as 1890 and scrapped only in 1960, could carry up to 1900 people upstream at 15.5 kph. At lower right, passing the sandstone mountains along the Elbe, is the *Schandau*, built at the Blasewitz yards in 1892 and equipped with new superstructures and renamed *Bad Schandau* in 1928; she measured 56 meters long, could carry 700 passengers, and was scrapped in 1980.

The color photo at left shows the Patria (see page 164) on her maiden voyage in 1938, a cruise to Norway, in harbor at Hammerfest.

Above: On June 24, 1929 the Bremen (51,656 tons, 286 meters overall, 846 passengers in first class, 515 in second, 300 in tourist and 617 in third), is seen leaving the AG "Weser" shipyard, her masts bristling with antennas, towed by several tugboats past a crowd of many thousand spectators and to Bremerhaven. The stylish flat funnels were lengthened shortly afterward (see page 2), as passengers complained of smoke and soot on deck.

The four-screw turbine liner Bremen and her sister ship Europa (49,746 tons, 286 meters, 2242 passengers) were the biggest and fastest

German merchant ships in action between the two World Wars and brought the Norddeutsche Lloyd back into the leading group of passenger shipping firms in the world. The Europa was built by Blohm & Voss in 1930 but was delivered eleven months late because of a fire that almost completely destroyed the ship's interior while she was being finished. On her maiden voyage in July of 1929, the Bremen covered the 3164 nautical miles from Cherbourg to the Ambrose Lightship off New York in four days, 17 hours and 42 minutes, averaging 27.83 knots and winning the Blue Riband from the Mauretania. In March of 1930 the Europa set a new Atlantic speed record of 27.91 knots on her first voyage, and in June of 1933, after modifications to her

engines, the Bremen averaged 28.51 knots to win back the Blue Riband, only to lose it barely two months later to the Italian Rex. In regular line service, the Bremen and Europa ran at 26 to 26.5 knots, a speed that was exceeded only to make up lost time, for the ships were scheduled to reach New York from Bremerhaven in six days, from Southampton and Cherbourg in five. This ocean express service, which also included the slower Columbus, offered weekly departures from Europe to America and back.

The picture on the next two pages, taken from the deck of the Bremen, shows her meeting the Europa on the stormy North Atlantic.

149

The pictures above show the rooms on the main promenade deck of the *Bremen,* designed by the Bremen architect Rudolf Alexander Schröder; above is the first-class smoking room, below the second-class sitting room.

In addition to their avant-garde styling and record speeds, the *Bremen* and *Europa* made an impression with their on-board mail planes. One day before the liner docked in New York or Cherbourg, the plane was launched from a catapult, thus speeding the mail considerably. The *Bremen* left New York two days before the war began, reached the Russian port of Murmansk, and returned to Germany in December of 1939, breaking through the British blockade. She was burned out at Bremerhaven in March of 1941 after a young crewman had lit a fire, and was then scrapped. The picture below shows the *Europa* being brought to the Columbus Pier in Bremerhaven; her funnels had already been lengthened. The *Europa* spent the war years at Bremerhaven, then served as an American troop transport, was turned over to France in 1946, operated as the Atlantic liner *Liberté* as of 1950 and was scrapped at La Spezia in 1962.

Left: The physicist Albert Einstein makes music on his way home from America on the Hapag liner *Deutschland* in 1931. The picture below was taken in 1930 by the famous photographer Erich Salomon, who was killed at Auschwitz in 1944; he was the first to use small hand cameras for fast exposures inside rooms. This picture shows the three-deck-high first-class dining room of the *Europa*, designed by the Munich architect Paul Ludwig Troost. Right: The first-class smoking room of the *Columbus,* also decorated by Troost, during her maiden voyage.

These pictures show famous passengers on German passenger liners; at upper left, Hapag General Manager and former German Chancellor Wilhelm Cuno, Mrs. Walker, wife of the Mayor of New York, who christened the ship of the same name, and Captain Karl Graalfs in New York Harbor on April 11, 1927 after her maiden voyage. Upper right: Movie actress Lilian Harvey aboard the *Europa* with Captain Oskar Scharf. Lower left: Conductor Arturo Toscanini on the bridge of the *Bremen* with Captain Hagemann. Lower right: World champion boxer Max Schmeling returning from America. Above at upper left: Movie actor Emil Jannings with his wife Gussy Holl, en route to America for three years, on the *Albert Ballin* in 1926. Upper right: Marlene Dietrich on the way to her first Hollywood film roles, on the deck of the *Bremen* in 1930. Below: First-class passengers of the *Cap Arcona* celebrate crossing the equator.

Left: The 2436-ton, 89-meter turbine steamer *Roland* of the Norddeutsche Lloyd, built by Tecklenborg at Geestemünde in 1927, carried up to 2900 passengers from Bremerhaven and Wilhelmshaven to Helgoland at 18 knots. The picture shows her after being rebuilt in 1935, when the aft funnel was removed and the originally white hull was painted black. She sank off Narva in the Gulf of Finland while serving as a minelayer in April of 194 Oderwerke in 1935, was, at 5504 tons and 130 meters overall, the biggest, and at 18 knots the fastest ship in the East Prussian service. She belonged to the government transport ministry, was run by the Hapag, and could carry 2000 passengers plus 100 cars. The *Tannenberg* ran from Travemünde via Warnemünde, Binz and Swinemünde to Zoppot, Pillau and Memel, and the line was occasionally extended to Kiel and Helsinki. She sank while serving as a minelayer in July of 1941, along with the *Preussen* and the *Hansestadt Danzig* (see page 134), on a Swedish mine barrage off Oland.

Lower left: The motor ship *Preussen*, built for the state of Prussia by Auhgust Pahl in Hamburg-Finkenwerder in 1939 and run by the Hapag, served as a ferry for 300 people and 32 cars between Cuxhaven and Brunsbüttelkoog. She displaced 573 tons, was 45 meters long overall and made 12 knots. In 1946 she was acquired by the state of Niedersachsen, was named *Niedersachsen* and operated until 1952 by the Hadag, then by the Greifen-Reederei of Brunsbüttel until she was laid up in 1953. In 1958 the *Niedersachsen* returned to service on her old route for the "Seelotse" Ferry Service of Cuxhaven, acquired new superstructures and funnel in 1964, and was sold to Italy in 1968, being replaced by a new ferry of the same name.

Upper right: The 2400-ton, 94-meter twin-screw motor ship

Königin Luise, built by the Howaldt Works of Hamburg in 1934, performed resort service to Helgoland for the Hapag. It was the first Hapag ship to be welded instead of riveted, could carry 2000 deck passengers at 17 knots, was rebuilt as a minelayer in 1939 and sank off Helsinki in 1939 after hitting a mine.

Right: The Hapag resort ship *Helgoland,* built by the Lindenau-Werft in Memel, had a destroyer stern, unlike the yacht stern of the *Königin Luise,* and came into service a few weeks before the war began in 1939. At 2947 tons and 113 meters overall, she could carry 2000 passengers at 17 knots. Her turbo-electric engines operated two Voith-Schneider propellers. The *Helgoland* was the biggest ship ever equipped with such a powerplant but had problems with it. A barrack ship at Cuxhaven during the war, she was turned over to Great Britain in 1945 and sunk at sea, loaded with poison gas grenades, in 1948.

In 1935 three 21-knot East Asian steamers were delivered to the Lloyd: the curved-bow sister ships *Scharnhorst* (18,184 tons, 199 meters overall, 153 first-class and 155 tourist passengers) and *Gneisenau* (left) by the AG "Weser" and the somewhat smaller and straight-bowed *Potsdam*, originally ordered by the Hapag, by Blohm & Voss. The *Scharnhorst* and *Potsdam* had turbo-electric engines, the *Gneisenau* had turbines. They were prestige ships promoted by the government of the Reich to gain ascendancy in the East Asian service, but not to run economically. The *Scharnhorst* was sold to Japan in 1942 and sunk by an American submarine in the Yellow Sea in 1944 as the aircraft carrier *Jinyo*, the *Potsdam* turned over to Britain in 1945 and

scrapped in Pakistan in 1976, and the *Gneisenau* sank after hitting a mine near Gedser in 1943.

On the test run of the *Scharnhorst*, the first big passenger ship built after the Nazis came to power, Adolf Hitler came aboard at Bremerhaven; he had been present at her launching a year before. Hess, Ribbentrop, Reich Defense Minister von Blomberg, Admiral Raeder and the top Lloyd executives were also present. At right, Hitler greets crewmen on deck; above, the *Scharnhorst* greets the incoming "Kraft durch Freude" steamer *Der Deutsche*, formerly *Sierra Morena* (see page 117), whose passengers had to take positions on deck "to thank the Führer for the nice trip", whereupon the ship, as is very clear in the picture, developed a list to starboard.

The Deutsche Ost-Afrika-Linie and the Woermann-Linie put two luxurious passenger ships, the *Pretoria* (right) and the *Windhuk* (left), into service in 1936 and 1937 to catch up with British and Italian competition on the Capetown route. These twin-screw turbine steamers of 16,662 tons and 178 meters were built by Blohm & Voss, made 18 knots and had accommodations for 152 passengers in first class and 369 in tourist. During the war the *Pretoria* lay at Pillau; she was turned over to Great Britain in 1945 and sold to Indonesia in 1964, where she has been used as a naval barrack ship since 1979. The *Windhuk* was confiscated by Brazil at Santos in 1942, sold to the U.S. Navy, and scrapped in the USA in 1966.

The Nazi "Kraft durch Freude" organization, a subsidiary of the "Deutscher Arbeiterfront" founded by the Nazis in 1933 after the labor unions were broken up, offered low-priced vacation trips for working-class people as of 1934, originally with chartered one-class ships. The first ship owned by the KdF was *Der Deutsche* (see page 161), which went into service in 1935, and it was decided in 1936 to contract for new KdF ships, only two of which were finished before the war. In 1938 the 1463-passenger *Wilhelm Gustloff* (left center), built by Blohm & Voss and run by the Hamburg-Süd, went into service, followed in 1939 by the 1766-passenger *Robert Ley* (lower left), built by the Howaldtswerke of Hamburg and run by the Hapag. The latter, at 27,188 tons and 204 meters long overall, had Diesel-electric engines and a speed of 15.5 knots. During the war she was used as a hospital and barrack ship at Gdingen, brought refugees westward early in 1945, was burned out in a bomb attack at Hamburg, and was scrapped in Britain in 1947. The 25,484-ton, 209-meter, 15.5-knot motor ship *Wilhelm Gustloff* also spent most of the war at Gdingen. On January 30, 1945 it left there and headed west with 6100 refugees and wounded. Late that evening, three torpedoes from a Russian U-boat struck the *Wilhelm Gustloff* in the Stolpmünde area; she

began to sink and capsized in an hour. Only 904 survivors were rescued; 5200 people died in the icy waters. Other terrible catastrophes followed in the last months of the war, including the sinking of the *Steuben* (3000 lost), the freighter *Goya* (7000 lost), and the *Cap Arcona* (5000 lost). They were the four largest losses in the history of shipping disasters.

Right: The three-screw steamer *Pennland*, launched by Harland & Wolff in 1920 as the *Pittsburgh* (16,082 tons, 183 meters long overall, 15 knots), came under the German flag in 1935 with her sister ship *Westernland* when the Hamburg shipowner Arnold Bernstein bought the Belgian Red Star Line and moved its headquarters to Hamburg. These ships, carrying 486 tourist-class passengers, ran between Antwerp and America. The Jewish Bernstein was arrested by the Gestapo in 1937, the Red Star Line "aryanized" and dissolved in 1939 after the ships were sold.

In 1933 the Hapag put two motor ships built by Blohm & Voss into service on the Central American route, the 12,049-ton *Cariba* and *Cordillera*, from whose deck her sister ship is seen here in the Atlantic, The twin-screw *Cariba* and *Cordillera* were 160 meters long overall made 17 knots, and could carry 234 passengers in first class, 103 in tourist and 110 in third. The *Cariba* was turned over to the USA in 1945, then to the USSR in 1946; the *Cordillera* sank at Swinemünde in 1945 during an air raid and was raised by the Russians in 1949. Both ran for some thirty years between Vladivostok and the Kamchatka Peninsula.

The last large passenger ship put into service by the Hapag before the war was the *Patria* (see picture on page 148), built by the Deutsche Werft in Hamburg-Finkenwerder and equipped with Diesel-electric engines. At 16,595 tons and 182 meters overall, she carried 185 passengers in first class, 164 in tourist, and made 17 knots. Before she entered line service through the Panama Canal and down the west coast of South America to Valparaiso, she made her maiden voyage to Norway. During the war she was first at Stettin, then at Flensburg as of 1941; she was turned over to Britain in 1945 and served as a Russian passenger ship on the Black Sea as of 1946, until she was scrapped in Pakistan in 1985.

Of the 131 German overseas passenger ships existing when the war began, 101 were sunk, wrecked, confiscated or sold, and the other thirty, in more or less damaged condition, had to be turned over the victors. Once again an irresponsible German war policy destroyed Germany's merchant fleet.

One of the 2830 wrecks left in Hamburg harbor after the war was the *Vaterland,* shown at right during scrapping on October 27, 1948. Bombs had struck her in July of 1943, tearing up her bow and decks. She had never officially been given her name, but had been launched hastily by Blohm & Voss on August 24, 1940 to free the slipway for U-boat construction. She was to be one of three 41,000-ton, 250-meter, 23.5-knot turbo-electric ships intended to replace the Hapag's *Albert Ballin* Class in the North Atlantic service. Now she was the last passenger ship ever contracted for by the Hapag.

After the war, German shipbuilding and shipping were put under stringent restrictions; only in 1951 the did rebuilding of the merchant fleet begin, and as of the mid-fifties, a few German shipping firms put large passenger ships back into service, most of which already had a long career behind them.

In 1955 the Europa-Canada-Linie, founded that same year in Bremen, placed the 12,575-ton, 150-meter motor ship *Seven Seas* in service between Bremerhaven and Montreal. It had been built as a freighter by Sun Shipbuilding of Chester, Pennsylvania in 1940, used as an aircraft carrier by the U.S. Navy as of 1941,

and then rebuilt into a passenger ship in 1949. The *Seven Seas* made 16 knots and carried 20 passengers in first class, 987 in tourist. She also made voyages to New York as well as cruises. In 1966 she was sold to Rotterdam and replaced by the *Ryndam*, which remained under the German flag for only one year. The picture above shows the *Seven Seas* at Aden during a world cruise that took her to Egypt, Ceylon, Australia, New Zealand and through the South Seas and the Panama Canal to the Caribbean and New York between October 1960 and March 1961.

Right: The 1808-ton, 78-meter, 13-knot *Nordland* was built for Danish

owners by Burmeister & Wain of Copenhagen in 1930 and bought by the Lübeck-Linie; after being rebuilt in 1957, she was used for Baltic and Norwegian cruises from Travemünde until she was sold to Finland in 1970.

The *Gripsholm* was the world's largest motor ship when she was built by Armstrong, Whitworth & Co. of Newcastle for the Svenska Amerika Linjen of Göteborg in 1925. In 1954

she was transferred to the Bremen-Amerika Linie, in which the Swedish line and the Norddeutsche Lloyd held equal shares. With a white hull, yellow Lloyd funnels and a German crew, she performed North Atlantic service as of February 1954, the first German passenger liner in almost 15 years. In January of 1955 she was taken over by the Lloyd, renamed *Berlin,* and her hull was painted

black. The 18,600-ton, 180-meter, 16-knot *Berlin* regularly carried up to 98 passengers in first class and 878 in tourist from Bremerhaven to New York and back, but was also used as a cruise ship. At the end of 1966 she was taken to La Spezia and scrapped. The picture above shows the *Berlin* in the English Channel near Dover.

Above: The *Hamburg* was one of six combination freighters of almost 9000 tons, 164 meters long overall, that had accommodations for 87 first-class passengers, made 17 knots, and were used in joint Hapag-Lloyd service to East Asia. The *Schwaben-stein* and *Hessenstein*, originally used by a branch of the Lloyd, and the Hapag ships *Hamburg* and *Frankfurt* went into service in 1954, with the *Bayernstein* and *Hannover* following in 1955. All six motor ships were built by Vulkan of Bremen and were sold to a Hong Kong shipping group in 1966-67.

Right center: The only Hapag passenger ship after the war was the 7505-ton, 138-meter, 18.5-knot turbine steamer *Ariadne*, which took 300 first-class passengers on cruises as of February 1958 and was sold to the USA in 1960. She had been built for the Svenska lloyd in Göteborg by Swan, Hunter & Wigham Richardson in Walker-on-Tyne in 1951 as the *Patricia*, bought by the Hapag in 1957 and renamed *Ariadne*.

Left: The Deutsche Bundesbahn's train ferry *Theodor Heuss*, built by the Howaldtswerke in Kiel, was the second ship to join the joint German-Danish line between Grossenbrode and Gedser. She joined the *Deutschland*, built in 1953, on what was originally only a freight line. The 5583-ton, 136-meter, 17-knot Diesel-electric ship *Theodor Heuss* had three tracks with a combined length of 317 meters and could carry up to 200 cars and 1500 people. After the Fehmarn Bridge was built, allowing rail connections via Lolland, the *Theodor Heuss* switched to the new "Vogelfluglinie" between Puttgarden and Rodbyhavn. In 1986 she was replaced by the *Karl Carstens* (see page 184), but still travels the same route as a train ferry, carrying no passengers.

The picture above shows the tourist-class sitting room of the Lloyd steamer *Bremen* of 1959 (see page 173).

In 1960 the DDR's first large passenger ship, the twin-screw motor ship *Völkerfreundschaft*, went into service. She had been built by the Götaverken of Göteborg in 1948 as the *Stockholm* and delivered to the Svenska Amerika Linjen, and had become famous by ramming and sinking the *Andrea Doria* in 1956. The 12,442-ton, 160-meter, 19-knot *Völkerfreundschaft* belonged to the Freier Deutscher Gewerkschaftsbund and was run by the VEB Deutsche Sdeereederei of Rostock. As a vacation ship, she was used on cruises for workers, of whom she could carry 568, and sometimes chartered to Western companies to earn her keep. She was sold to Panama in 1985.

The FDGB's second vacation ship was the *Fritz Heckert*, built by the Mathias-Thesen-Werft in Wismar. A twin-screw ship of 8120 tons, 141 meters long overall, she made 17 knots and had accommodations for 384 passengers. Her Diesel engines and gas turbines turned out to be troublesome, and so the *Fritz Heckert* was laid up in 1972. The picture at upper left shows her in Stralsund, where she is still in use as a barrack ship as of 1990.

Lower left: The 6164-ton, 137-meter, 18-knot *Sassnitz*, built by VEB Neptunwerft of Rostock in 1959, ran as the Deutsche Reichsbahn's train ferry between Sassnitz and Trelleborg. She carried four tracks with a total length of 380 meters and could carry 980 passengers and 25 cars. As of 1977 she was used only as a reserve ship.

The Hamburg-Atlantik-Linie, founded in January of 1958 by the Dane Axel Bitsch-Christensen, immediately bought the British Canadian Pacific's twin-screw turbine liner *Empress of Scotland*, built in 1930 by Fairfields of Glasgow. She had been the fastest transpacific liner, and had been called the *Empress of Japan* until 1942. She was rebuilt at the Howaldtswerke in Hamburg; the forward part of the superstructure was replaced by a modern front, the three tall funnels by two wider, lower ones, and a new stem had been installed. Now named *Hanseatic*, she set out on her maiden voyage from Hamburg and Cuxhaven to Southampton and New York on July 19, 1958. The 30,030-ton, 205-meter *Hanseatic*, running at a cruising speed of 20 knots, carried 85 first-class and 1167 tourist passengers in the North Atlantic service, but also made cruises, especially in winter, carrying only 750 passengers. In September of 1966

her engine room burned in New York; she was towed to Hamburg and, since it did not pay to repair her, she was scrapped by Eisen & Metall. The picture above shows the *Hanseatic* on a Norwegian cruise after her exhaust pipe was lengthened in 1962.

Upper left: The 32,336-ton, 212-meter, 23-knot four-screw turbine liner *Bremen* lies at a New York pier in July of 1959 after finishing her maiden voyage. In view of the financial success of the *Berlin*, the Norddeutsche Lloyd had decided to put another transatlantic liner in service, and since the cost of a new ship could not be calculated because of the long delivery times in the shipbuilding boom at the end of the fifties, they bought the French passenger liner *Pasteur* in 1957. She had been built for the South American trade by the Penhoet yards of St. Nazaire in 1939 but, what with World War II and the Indo-China War, had only been used as a troop transport. The *Pasteur* was

rebuilt by Vulkan of Bremen, gaining a modern funnel and completely new passenger accommodations (see page 169), and was renamed *Bremen* in 1959. The *Bremen*, now the ninth-largest passenger ship in the world, carried 216 first-class and 906 tourist passengers on the traditional route from Bremerhaven to New York and was also used for cruises. In 1971 the Hapag-Lloyd AG, in which the two largest German shipping firms had united the previous year, decided to give up their North Atlantic service in 1971 in view of the constantly decreasing numbers of passengers. The *Bremen* was sold to the Greek Chandris Line in January of 1972, but as of 1977 she was laid up at Jidda as the barrack ship *Saudiphil I* and sank in 1980 as the *Filipinas Saudia I* while being towed to Taiwan to be scrapped. The photo sequence at lower left shows the last minutes of the former *Bremen* in the Indian Ocean on June 9, 1980.

Above: The 6149-ton, 136-meter train ferry *Warnemünde* of the Deutsche Reichsbahn, built by the Neptunwerft of Rostock, has three tracks with a total length of 315 meters, can carry up to 140 cars and 800 passengers, and makes 18 knots. Since 1963 she has been running between Warnemünde and Gedser.

Left center: The first *Nils Holgersson* (3529 tons, 110 meters overall, 19 knots), built by the Hanseatische Werft in Hamburg-Harburg, could carry 650 passengers and 90 cars and opened service between Travemünde and Trelleborg for the TT-Linie of Hamburg in March of 1962. When the second *Nils Holgersson* was launched in 1966, she was renamed *Gösta Berling*, sold to France in 1967 and registered in Cyprus in 1973. In 1975 she returned to the German flag as the *Mary Poppins*.

Lower left: The *Regina Maris* (5813 tons, 118 meters overall, 20 knots), was delivered to the Lübeck-Linie by the Flenderwerke of Lübeck in 1966 and made voyages with up to 276 passengers until she was sold to Canada in 1976. From 1980 to 1983 she ran for another German ship-owner, Peter Deilmann, though she was registered in Singapore.

Below: In October of 1965 the Norddeutsche Lloyd purchased the *Kungsholm*, built in 1953 by the "De Schelde" yards in Vlissingen, from the Svenska Amerika Linjen of Göteborg and renamed her *Europa*. The 21,514-ton, 183-meter twin-screw motor ship, with a cruising speed of 19 knots, was intended to replace the *Berlin*, which was taken out of service a year later, and made her first voyage from Bremerhaven to Berlin in January of 1966. The *Europa*, which could carry up to 122 first-class and 721 tourist passengers, provided regular North Atlantic service but had been conceived from the start as a cruise ship, for the days of passenger liners running between Europe and America were nearing their end. Whereas a good million people had crossed the Atlantic by ship in 1962, by 1970 there were fewer than a quarter million, and at the same time the number of airplane passengers had grown from two million to more than eight. At the end of 1971 the Hapag-Lloyd gave up its tradition-rich Atlantic line service. The *Bremen* was sold, while the *Europa* was given a new coat of white paint with blue and yellow stripes on her hull, her funnels were painted with the new "HL" logo, and from then on she made only cruises. In the autumn of 1981 she was sold to the Italian Costa Line; as the *Columbus C*, she rammed a pier at Cadiz in 1984 and was scrapped in 1985. The picture shows the *Europa* in New York while still an Atlantic liner.

The picture at the left shows vacationers on the afterdeck of the *Astor* (see page 186).

Above: On the lower Weser, the cruise ship *Europa* meets the *Roland von Bremen*, which is returning from Helgoland. The latter was built in Helsingör as a Danish banana freighter in 1939 and bought by the Bremen resort service of D. Oltmann in 1965 to replace the wrecked *Bremerhaven*. She was rebuilt as a resort ship at Genoa and, beginning in 1966, she carried up to 1900 passengers between Bremerhaven and Helgoland. The 4391-ton, 114-meter, 16-knot *Roland von Bremen* was replaced in 1985 by the *Helgoland* (ex *Alte Liebe* ex *Wappen* ex *Wappen von Hamburg*) and scrapped at Bremen.

On December 22, 1980 the largest German passenger ship since World War II was launched and christened *Europa* by Simone Weil, the President of the European Parliament. The Vulkan of Bremen delivered the 33,819-ton, 200-meter, 21-knot twin-screw motor ship to Hapag-Lloyd in December of 1981, which sent it on its maiden voyage in January of 1982. The *Europa*, fitted with roomy and luxurious accommodations for 600 passengers (see page 180), still ranks as one of the world's favorite cruise ships in 1990.

Above: The first *Wappen von Hamburg* (2496 tons, 90 meters overall, 18 knots), built by Blohm & Voss in 1955, carried up to 1600 passengers between Hamburg and Helgoland for the Hadag and was sold to Greece in 1961.

Left: The *Atlantis* (243 tons, 46 meters overall, 12.5 knots), built at the Jadewerft in Wilhelmshaven for the Cuxhaven firm of Cassen Eils, carried up to 465 passengers from various islands and mainland ports to Helgoland and also carried supplies from Cuxhaven to that island during the winter months. In 1964 she was lengthened by four meters, now made 14 knots and displaced 348 tons. In 1972 she was sold to a firm in Panama.

The picture at lower left shows the *Rüm Hart* (373 tons, 49 meters overall, 12.5 knots), built by the Husumer Schiffwerft for the Wyker Dampf-schiffsreederei, on her test run on May 13, 1959. She was an enlarged version of the *Uthlande* and *Schleswig-Holstein,* which were put into service in 1955 and 1958, and performed line service from Dagebüll to Föhr and Amrum, as well as to Helgoland, with eight to ten cars on her fore- and afterdeck and up to 660 passengers. In 1960 she was the line's first ship to have her hull painted white; in 1970, after island traffic was switched to car ferries, she was used only for excursions. In 1982 the *Rüm Hart* was sold to Neustadt, in 1983 to Kappeln, and she is still in use as a "butter steamer" on the Baltic.

Upper right: The *Seute Deern* (640 tons, 58 meters overall, 15 knots), built by the Nordseewerke of Emden for Cassen Eils of Cuxhaven, is still carrying up to 764 passengers from various mainland and island ports to Helgoland. The picture shows her after being rebuilt in 1979, when she gained six meters and 129 tons.

Right center: The *Wilhelmshaven* (1588 tons, 76 meters, 19 knots), built by the Rolandwerft of Bremen, has been running since 1963, first for the Schiffahrtsgesellschaft "Jade", as of 1986 for the Harle-Reederei, carrying up to 1100 passengers from Wilhelmshaven to Helgoland.

Below: The third *Wappen von Hamburg* (4438 tons, 110 meters overall, 21.5 knots), built by Howaldt of Hamburg in 1965 for the Hadag's Hamburg-Helgoland service, ran only from Cuxhaven to Helgoland as of the early eighties and was sold in 1984 to the Flensburger Seetouristik, which still runs her on the same route.

The pictures on the next two pages show, at left, the reception hall of the cruise ship *Europa* of 1981 (see page 177), and at right, the post-modern discotheque aboard the Channel ferry *Olau Hollandia* of 1989 (see page 189).

Upper left: To replace the burned-out *Hanseatic* (see page 173), the firm that had meanwhile become the Deutsche Atlantik Linie bought the Israeli two-screw turbine ship *Shalom*, which had been built by the Chantiers de l'Atlantique at St. Nazaire in 1964, and put it on the North Atlantic route as the new *Hanseatic*. The 25,320-ton *Hanseatic*, 191 meters overall, with a 20-knot cruising speed, had room for 650 passengers; she was used only for cruises as of 1969, then sold to the Home Lines of Panama in July of 1973 as the *Doric*, and is still afloat as of 1990 as the Greek *Royal Odyssee*. The picture at lower left shows the 25,022-ton, 195-meter, 22-knot twin-screw turbine steamer *Hamburg*, the first large passenger ship built new in Germany since the war, at the overseas pier in its hope port. It was launched at the Deutsche Werft in Hamburg-Finkenwerder on February 21, 1968 and put into service by the Deutsche Atlantik Linie as a 652-passenger cruise ship. In the early seventies, as the dollar fell steadily and the line's payroll rose, the *Hanseatic* had to be sold in July of 1973, and in September the *Hamburg* was renamed Hanseatic. When the oil crisis suddenly drove fuel costs sky-high, the Deutsche Atlantik Linie ended its shipping activities and sold the *Hanseatic* (ex *Hamburg*). In January of 1974 she went back into service as the Russian *Maksim Gorkij*, and still makes cruises under this name.

The picture below shows one of the typical Rhine ships of the sixties and seventies passing the Pfalz at Kaub; she is the *Deutschland*, delivered to the Köln-Düsseldörfer Rhein-schiffahrt by Berninghaus of Köln-Deutz in 1961. This ship, 91 meters long overall and powered by two Voith-Schneider side propellers, can carry 3200 passengers; she was rebuilt after a fire in 1968 and renamed *Drachenfels* in 1968 and *Wappen von Mainz* in 1971.

After a new *Deutschland* had replaced her namesake of 1953 in 1972, the *Theodor Heuss* (see page 168) was replaced by the railroad ferry *Karl Carstens* on the Vogelfluglinie. This 12,830-ton, 18-knot Diesel-electric ferry, built by the Howaldts-werke-Deutsche Werft in Kiel, is 165 meters long overall, has three tracks with a total length of 405 meters, and can carry 1500 passengers and up to 333 cars. As can be seen, train ferries are often noticeably narrow in comparison to their length, not only because the railroad cars have to be housed within the hull, but also because the Vogelfluglinie berths at Puttgarden and Rödbyhavn limit the width of the ship to 17.7 meters.

Right: The ferry *Vikingfjord* (3815 tons, 108 meters overall, 22 knots), built for the Nordlandfähre-Reederei of Cuxhaven by the Meyerwerft of Papenburg in 1969, ran between Cuxhaven and Norway at first, then was chartered by the Prinzenlinie and operated by the Hadag and named *Prinz Hamlet II*, succeeding the first *Prinz Hamlet* and carrying 900 passengers between Hamburg and Harwich as of the end of 1970. When the third *Prinz Hamlet* was put into service in 1974, she was sold to Algeria.

Right: In 1972 the Hadag obtained the new *Westerland* from the Mützelfeldtwerft of Cuxhaven to replace the *Gorch Fock*, which had been built in 1963. In 1977 she became the *Stadt Kiel II* and ran under the flag of the Kieler Verkehrs AG, then was sold in 1979, as *Heimatland I*, to Willy Freter of Heiligenhafen. This picture shows her late in May of 1990 as the *Pidder Ling* (999 tons, 68 meters overall, 18 knots) of the Wyker Dampfschiffs-Reederei Föhr-Amrum, by whom she was bought in December of 1981 to replace the *Rüm Hart* (see page 178). Since then she has been used for excursions, especially to Helgoland, carrying up to 800 passengers.

Right: The third *Prinz Hamlet* (5830 tons, 119 meters overall, 22 knots), built by the Nobiskrugwerft of Rendsburg and run by the Hadag, served as a ferry between Hamburg and Harwich, carrying up to 1100 passengers and 210 cars. In 1981 the Danish DFDS took over her operation, and in April of 1987 to *Prinz Hamlet* was replaced by the *Hamburg*, no longer running under the German flag.

Above: On December 16, 1980 the Hamburg yards of the HDW launched the twin-screw motor ship *Astor* (18,835 tons, 164 meters overall, 18 knots). A year later, equipped for 638 passengers, she went into service as a cruise ship for the Hadag Cruise Line (see page 176). The *Astor* lost millions and was sold to South Africa at the end of 1983 without having her name changed. In 1985 the VEB Deutfracht-Seereederei bought the ship to replace the *Völkerfreundschaft* (see page 171), renamed her *Arkona,* and put her into service under the East German flag. This picture shows the *Arkona,* still calling Rostock her home, leaving Warnemünde in 1990.

Right: The cruise ship *Berlin* (7812 tons, 123 meters overall, 19 knots), built by the HDW in Kiel for the Reederei Peter Deilmann in Neustadt, was lengthened 17 meters in 1986, raising her tonnage to 9570 and her passenger capacity from 330 to 470. She is still in service as of 1990.

Lower right: The third *Nils Holgersson* (12,515 tons, 149 meters overall, 22 knots), delivered to the TT-Linie by the Nobiskrugwerft of Rendsburg in 1975, and her sister ship, the second *Peter Pan,* were then the largest Baltic ferries and ran between Travemünde and Trelleborg, as of 1981 in joint service of the TT-Linie and Saga Linjen. The *Nils Holgersson* could carry 1600 passengers, 712 of them in cabins, and 470 cars, and was sold to Australia in 1984.

186

Upper right: The *Käpt'n Brass* (859 tons, 58 meters overall, 15 knots), built for KG Seetouristik of Flensburg by the Jadewerft of Wilhelmshaven in 1979, ran on the Baltic as an excursion ship and "butter steamer" for 825 passengers, with Burgstaaken as her home port. In May of 1990 she was sold to Iran and renamed *Iran Hormuz 2*.

The picture at the right center, taken in the summer of 1987, shows the *Frisia II* (828 tons, 53 meters overall, 12 knots), built by Jos. L. Meyer of Papenburg for the AG Reederei Norden-Frisia of Norden in 1978, which still runs between Norddeich and the islands of Juist and Norderney as of 1990, carrying up to 1340 passengers in summer, 500 passengers and 35 cars in winter.

Below: The *Uthlande* (923 tons, 58 meters overall, 12.5 knots), built by the Husumer Schiffwerft for the Wyker Dampfschiffsreederei, came into ferry service in April of 1980 as the sister ship of the *Nordfriesland*, built in 1978, running between Dagebüll and the islands of Föhr and Amrum, carrying 975 passengers and 45 cars. This picture, taken on May 27, 1990, shows the *Uthlande* after being lengthened to 68 meters at the Meyerwerft in Papenburg, which raised her tonnage to 999 and her capacity to 55 cars.

Left: The *Olau Britannia* (14,985 tons, 153 meters overall, 21 knots), built by the Seebeckwerft of Bremerhaven in 1982 for the Olau-Linie of Hamburg, a branch of the TT-Linie, and her sister ship *Olau Hollandia*, finished a year before, could carry 1600 passengers and 550 cars and ran between Vlissingen and Sheerness, England, before being replaced by two new ships with the same names in 1989 and 1990.

Below: The third *Peter Pan*, delivered to the TT-Linie of Hamburg by the Seebeckwerft of Bremerhaven on May 30, 1986, and her sister ship, the fourth *Nils Holgersson*, which runs under the Swedish flag, are still providing ferry service between Travemünde and Trelleborg in 1990.

The *Peter Pan*, 161 meters long overall with a gross space rating of 31,360, which represents some 22,000 tons, can carry 550 cars as well as some 1600 passengers, including 1322 people in 489 cabins.

Above: The first large German passenger ship of the nineties is the *Olau Britannia*, built by the Schichau Seebeckwerft in Bremerhaven for the Olau-Linie of Hamburg, which began line service from Vlissingen to Sheerness on May 21, 1990. She serves this route along with her sister ship, the second *Olau Hollandia*, which went into service in 1989. Both ferries

are 161 meters long overall, make 21.5 knots and have a gross space rating of 33,336, can transport 575 cars and offer 1642 beds in 423 cabins and 78 more in 13 economy units. As on the *Europa* (see page 177), the public rooms no longer extend the whole length of the ship but are concentrated on three decks, one over another, toward the stern, while the forward part of the superstructure is occupied by the hotel cabins. In the post-modern interiors of the *Olau Britannia* and her sister ship are seven hundred mirrors with a total area of a thousand square meters, five hundred

square meters of marble and granite flooring, five hundred mirrored flower and palm-tree boxes, and chrome and glass everywhere. The imposing interiors of these jumbo ferries, with their lavishly furnished foyers, halls, galleries and arcades, restaurants, swimming pools, and discotheques, equal the luxury formerly offered by the finest trans-atlantic liners, and in terms of size, these representatives of a new generation of ferries are among the world's largest ships as the turn of the century approaches.

Index of Ships' Names

This index lists the names of all ships mentioned in the book. The year in parentheses is that in which the ship was turned over to her owners by her builders, or in the case of renamed ships, the year in which she was given that name. For ships bought from outside Germany, the year is that in which the ship with that name came under the German flag. For ships built for German firms but not put into service, or not into German service, the year of launching is usually omitted.

Bibliography

Althof, Wolfgang, *Passagiere an Bord*, Rostock 1988.

Baker, William A., *Vom Raddampfer zum Atomschiff. Geschichte der maschinengetriebenen Schiffe.* Bielefeld & Berlin 1966.

Benja, Günter, *150 Jahre Bremer Seebädertörns 1837-1987*, Bremen 1989.

Benja, Günter, *Personenschiffahrt in deutschen Gewässern*, Oldenburg & Hamburg 1975.

Bessell, Georg, & August Westermann. *150 Jahre Schiffbau in Vegesack*, Bremen 1955.

Blumenschein, Ulrich, *Luxusliner, Glanz und Ende der grossen Passagierschiffe des Atlantiks*, Oldenburg & Hamburg 1975.

Bock, Bruno, *Gebaut bei HDW, Howaldtswerke-Deutsche Werft AG 150 Jahre*, Herford 1988.

Bocking, Werner, *Die Geschichte der Rheinschiffahrt, Schiffe auf dem Rhein in drei Jahrtausenden*, Moers 1980.

Bonsor, Noel R.P., *North Atlantic Seaway*, 5 Vol., Newton Abbot & Jersey 1975-1980.

Borger-Keweloh, Nicola, Reisen, *Lustfahrten und Triumphzüge - Ein Kölner Patrizier auf dem Rhein*, in: Deutsche Schiffahrt 1/89.

Bracker, Jörgen & Carsten Prange (Eds.), Alster, *Elbe und die See. Hamburgs Schiffahrt und Hafen in Gemälden, Zeichnungen und Aquarellen des Museums für Hamburgische Geschichte*, Hamburg 1981.

Brinnin, John Malcolm & Kenneth Gaulin, *Grand Hotels der Meere. Die goldene Ära der Luxusliner*, Munich 1988.

Bundgen, Eduard, *Die Personenschiffahrt auf dem Rhein. Vom Schaufelraddampfer zum Kabinenschiff*, Freiburg 1987.

Detlefsen, Gert Uwe, *Flensburger Förde-Schiffe*, Herford 1977.

Detlefsen, Gert Uwe, *Flensburger Schiffbau-Gesellschaft 1872-1982. 110 Jahre Schiffbau in Flensburg*, Hamburg 1982.

Detlefsen, Gert Uwe, *1885-1985. 100 Jahre Wyker Dampfschiffs-Reederei Föhr-Amrum GmbH). Chronik einer Inselreederei*, 2nd ed., no place, 1985.

Detlefsen, Gert Uwe, H. Schuldt, *Flensburg-Hamburg. Chronik einer Reederei*, Bad Segeberg & Hamburg 1988.

Deppert, Werner, *Mit Dampfmaschine und Schaufelrad. Die Dampfschiffahrt auf dem Bodensee 1817-1967*, Konstanz 1975.

Dunn, Laurence, *Famous Liners of the Past, Belfast Built*, London 1964.

Frick, Curt, *Autofähren und Passagierschiffe der Welt*, Zürich 1975.

Frick, Curt, *Passagierschiffe und Autofähren der Welt*, Zürich 1967.

Gerdau, Kurt, *Seedienst Ostpreussen*, Herford 1990.

Gröber, Roland, *Maximilian. Die Geschichte des ersten Dampfschiffes auf dem Starnberger See. In: Vom Einbaum zum Dampfschiff, Jahrbuch des Fördervereins Südbayerisches Schiffahrtsmuseum Starnberg*, Starnberg 1981.

Groggert, Kurt, *Personenschiffahrt auf Spree und Havel*, Berlin 1988.

Hader, Arnulf & Günther Meier, *Eisenbahnfähren der Welt. Vom Trajekt zur Dreideckfähre*, Herford 1986.

Hansen, Clas Broder, *Dampfarchitektur*, in: Volker Plagemann (ed.), Ubersee. *Seeschiffahrt und Seemacht im deutschen Kaiserreich*, Munich 1988.

Hansen, Hans Jürgen, *Schiffe, Häfen, Meere und Matrosen. Eine Geschichte der Schiffahrt und des Seeverkehrs. Oldenburg & Hamburg 1975.

Hansen, Sönke, *Adolf Hitler war zweimal in Bremerhaven*, in: Niederdeutsches Heimatblatt No. 459, March 1988.

Heinsius, Paul, *Der Ubergang zum Maschinenantrieb und vom Holz-zum Eisenschiffbau an den deutschen Ost- und Nordseeküsten im 19. Jahrhundert*, in: Deutsches Schiffahrtsarchiv 1, Oldenburg & Hamburg 1975.

Hughes, Tom, *Der Kampf ums Blaue Band*, Oldenburg und Hamburg 1974.

Hieke, Ernst, Rob. M. Sloman Jr., *Errichtet 1793*, Hamburg 1968.

Isherwood, J.H., *Steamers of the Past*, Liverpool 1966.

Jaeger, Werner, *Das Mittelrad-Dampfschiff Prinzessin Charlotte von Preussen, 1816*, Oldenburg & Hamburg 1977.

Kludas, Arnold, *Deutsche Ozean-Passagierschiffe, 1850 bis 1895*, Moers 1983.

Kludas, Arnold, *Die Geschichte der deutschen Passagierschiffahrt*, 5 Vol., Hamburg 1986-1990.

Kludas, Arnold, *Die grossen deutschen Passagierschiffe. Dokumentation in Wort und Bild*, Oldenburg & Hamburg 1971.

Kludas, Arnold, *Die grossen Passagierschiffe Fähren und Cruise-Liner der Welt*, Herford 1983.

Kludas, Arnold, *Die grossen Passagierschiffe der Welt*, Herford 1987.

Kludas, Arnold, *Die Schiffe der deutschen Afrika-Linien 1880-1945*, Oldenburg & Hamburg 1975.

Kludas, Arnold, *Die Schiffe der Hamburg-Süd 1871-1951*, Oldenburg & Hamburg 1976.

Kludas, Arnold, *Hundert Jahre HADAG-Schiffe 1888-1988*, Herford 1988.

Kludas, Arnold & Herbert Vischoff, *Die Schiffe der Hamburg-Amerika Linie*, 3 Vol., Herford 1979-1981.

Köhnemann, Wilfried & Udo Burk, *Das Schiff. Eine Idee fährt zur See. Die Europa*, 2nd ed., no place, 1987.

Kresse, Walter, *Aus der Vergangenheit der Reiherstiegwerft in Hamburg*, Hamburg, no date.

Kresse, Walter, *Die Fahrtgebiete der Hamburger Handelsflotte 1824-1888*, Hamburg 1972.

Kresse, Walter, *Seeschiffs-Verzeichnis der Hamburger Reedereien 1824-1888*, 3 Vol., Hamburg 1969.

Kuke, Herbert, *Kurs Helgoland. Eine Geschichte des Seebades, des Seebäderdienstes und der Seebäderschiffe seit 1829*, Oldenburg & Hamburg 1974.

Lenz, Siegfried, *Die Wracks von Hamburg*, Oldenburg & Hamburg 1978.

Mathies, Otto, *Hamburgs Reederei 1814-1914*, Hamburg 1924.

McCaughan, Michael, *Steel Ships & Iron Men. Shipbuilding in Belfast, 1894-1912*, Belfast 1989.

Mertens, Eberhard (ed.), *Der Ozean-Express. Turbinenschnelldampfer Bremen des Norddeutschen Lloyd 1929-1941*, 2nd ed., Hildesheim 1976.

Mertens, Eberhard (ed.), *Die Hapag-Riesen der Imperator-Klasse*, Hildesheim 1974.

Michels, Walter, *Unvergessene Dampfschiffahrt auf Rhein und Donau*, Darmstadt 1967.

Miller, William H., *Famous Ocean Liners. The Story of Passenger Shipping, from the Turn of the Century to the Present Day*, Wellingborough 1987.

Miller, William H., *German Ocean Liners of the 20th Century*, Wellingborough 1987.

Miller, William H., *The Fabulous Interiors of the Great Ocean Liners*, New York 1985.

Müller, Frank & Wolfgang Quinger, *Mit Dampf und Schaufelrad auf der Oberelbe*, Berlin 1988.

Napp-Zinn, A.F., *Die ersten deutschen Rheindampfer*, Oberhausen 1938.

Niemz, Günter & Reiner Wachs, *Personenschiffahrt auf der Oberelbe*, Bielefeld 1981.

Oosten, F.C. van, *Dampfer erobern die Meere. Die Anfänge der Dampfschiffahrt*, Oldenburg & Hamburg 1975.

Pedersen, Peter, *Die grosse Zeit der Luxus-Liner*, 2nd ed., Hamburg 1986.

Plagemann, Volker (ed.), *Ubersee. Seefahrt und Seemacht im deutschen Kaiserreich*, Munich 1988.

Prager, Hans Georg, *Blohm & Voss. Schiffe und Maschinen für die Welt*, Herford 1977.

Rothe, Claus, *Deutsche Ozean-Passagierschiffe, 1896 bis 1918*, Moers 1986.

Rothe, Claus, *Deutsche Ozean-Passagierschiffe, 1919 bis 1985*, Moers 1987.

Rothe, Claus, *Deutsche Seebäderschiffe 1830 bis 1939*, Moers 1989.

Rohbrecht, Gerhard, *Die deutschen Fahrgestschiffe. Ein Register*, in: Schiffahrt international, December 1973 to June 1978.

Schmelzkopf, Reinhart, *Die deutsche Handelsschiffahrt 1919-1939*, 2 Vol., Oldenburg & Hamburg 1974-1975.

Schönfeld, Peter, *Die Hamburger Seebäder- und Fährschiffe von der Jahrhundertwende bis 1945*, Hamburg 1974.

Schönfeldt, Peter, *Die Hamburger Seebäder- und Fährschiffe 1945-1973*, Hamburg 1973.

Seiler, Otto J., *Australienfahrt. Linienschiffahrt der Hapag-Lloyd AG im Wandel der Zeiten*, Herford 1988.

Seiler, Otto J., *Nordamerikafahrt. Linienschiffahrt der Hapag-Lloyd AG im Wandel der Zeiten*, Herford 1990.

Seiler, Otto J., *Ostasienfahrt. Linienschiffahrt der Hapag-Lloyd AG im Wandel der Zeiten*, Herford 1988.

Stolz, Gerd, *Die Cap Arcona-Katastrophe vom 3. Mai 1945*, in: Schleswig-Holstein, May 1990.

Szymanski, Hans, *Die Anfänge der Dampfschiffahrt in Niedersachsen und in den angrenzenden Gebieten von 1817 bis 1867*, Hannover 1958.

Trost, Heinz, *Die Lauenburger Dampfschiffe und ihre Nachfolger*, Wesselburen & Hamburg 1975.

Trost, Heinz, *Zwischen Havel, Spree und Dahme. Aus der Geschichte der Berliner Fahrgastschiffahrt*, Wesselburen & Hamburg 1979.

Vehrs/Heinsohn, T.S., *Hanseatic. Die Geschichte einer "Schönen Hamburgerin,"* Cuxhaven 1988.

Wagner, Frank, *Zwischen Hamburg und Stade, Ein Kapitel aus der Niederelb-Dampfschiffahrt*, Wesselburen & Hamburg 1970.

Witthöft, Hans Jürgen, *Hapag Hamburg-Amerika Linie*, Herford 1973.

Witthöft, Hans Jürgen, *Hapag-Lloyd: Uber ein Jahrhundert weltweite deutsche Seeschiffahrt im Bild*, Herford 1974.

Witthöft, Hans Jürgen, *Norddeutscher Lloyd*, Herford 1973.

Wölfer, Joachim, *Cap Arcona. Biographie eines Schiffes, Geschichte einer Reederei*. Herford 1977.

Wulle, Armin, *Der Stettiner Culcan*, Herford 1989.

Anonymous, *Die Schiffahrt auf dem Bodensee und Rhein. 150 Jahre Kursschiffahft*, Karlsruhe, no date.